BYZANTINE AESTHETICS

: ὑ̔πομνημεὶς
τὸ ν ἅ̓ΓΙ ΟΝ ἀ̓πο
φ̔ολον καὶ έ̓γας
Γελὶ θὴ νἰ ω̃ καὶ
θεολοΓΟΝ :·

Byzantine Aesthetics

Gervase Mathew

Icon Editions
Harper & Row, Publishers
New York, Evanston, San Francisco, London

TO

DAVID MATHEW

UNICO FRATRI AMICO OPTIMO

This book was first published in 1964 by The Viking Press, Inc. First Icon Edition published 1971.

STANDARD BOOK NUMBER: 06-435566-7

LIBRARY OF CONGRESS CATALOG CARD NUMBER: 64-12098

Contents

Foreword   xiii

Byzantine Aesthetics   1

The Third-Century Transition   12

The Mathematical Setting   23

The Hidden Meaning   38

The Phase of Integration   48

The Age of Justinian   62

The Official Programme   78

The Evolution of the Image   94

Amorians and Macedonians   108

The Macedonian Renaissance   122

Comnenians and Palaeologans   135

The Harmony of Colours   142

The Succession in the Imperial Sovereignty 162

Notes   165

Bibliography   179

Index   181

Illustrations

1   St John on Patmos. St John is dictating to St   *Front.*
    Prochoros on the island of Patmos. This illumination
    is from the first book of the *Lives* by Simeon Meta-
    phrastes. The most probable date is between 1081 and
    1118. (British Museum Add. MS. 11870, fol. 197b.)

                                                         facing
2   The Conquest of Death. Detail of the Anastasis,   2
    a wall-painting uncovered in the parecclesion of the
    church of the Chora at Constantinople. It is of the
    14th century, perhaps between 1320 and 1340.

3   The Virgin of Torcello. The Virgin in the apse   3
    of the cathedral of Torcello, close to Venice, is almost
    certainly Constantinopolitan work of the Early Com-
    nenian period. Through its sense of time and its
    utilization of space it reflects the new geometric fashion.

4   The Dance of Cybele and the Seasons. A   18
    silver disk of the late 3rd or early 4th century A.D.
    found at Parabiago and now in the Pinacoteca di Brera
    at Milan.

5   The Imperial Image. The date and provenance of   19
    this porphyry head in Venice, at the corner of the
    basilica of San Marco, has been much disputed. It
    seems most likely that it is late 3rd century and from
    Alexandria and represents a junior member of Dio-
    cletian's first Tetrarchy.

6   Christ upon the Paten. This paten for use in the   34
    eucharistic liturgy is in jewelled and enamelled ala-
    baster; it is preserved in the Treasury of San Marco.
    It is Constantinopolitan and of the late 10th or early
    11th century.

Illustrations

7 THE PLEDGE OF INCORRUPTION. Peacocks on the   35
chancel screen of the cathedral of Torcello. This is
Constantinopolitan work, most probably of the period
between 1081 and 1143. Since peacock's flesh was held
to be incorruptible, the scene represents the Christian
gaining incorruption by partaking of the Chalice.

8 THE IMPERIAL LITURGY. A silver disk now in the   50
Academia de la Historia at Madrid. It represents
Theodosius I enthroned and was commissioned to
celebrate the Decennalia of 388. It is possibly from
Thessalonika.

9 THE IMPERIAL PRESENCE. A later image of   51
Theodosius I, carved on the base of a column in the
Hippodrome at Constantinople, represents the alternative convention in the representation of Imperial
sovereignty. On the silver disk (Plate 8) this was
shown in action; here, only its presence is indicated;
but in both, Sovereignty is seen as dominant over its
setting.

10 THE EMPEROR IN TRIUMPH. An ivory leaf of an   66
Imperial diptych from Constantinople now at Paris in
the Musée du Louvre. It is almost certain that it represents the Emperor Justinian (527–565).

11 PASTORAL. A silver dish found at Klimova in South   67
Russia and now in the Hermitage Museum at Leningrad. It can be placed and dated through the silver
control stamps as being made at Constantinople
between 527 and 565.

12 THE CHURCH OF ST VITALIS. San Vitale at Ravenna   82
seems to represent one of the points of fusion between
traditions of ecclesiastical and secular building during
the age of Justinian: that of the Christian church and
of the audience hall in an Imperial palace. It is all the
more representative since the surviving mosaics are so
clearly part of its architecture.

Illustrations

13 THE THRONE OF MAXIMIAN. It can be taken as established that this throne was carved at a workshop in 6th-century Constantinople. Probably, it was sent as an Imperial Benefaction by Justinian to Maximian, Bishop of Ravenna.   83

14 CHRIST ENTHRONED AMONG HIS APOSTLES. A Byzantine carving most probably of the 7th century, now on the outer wall of San Marco in the Piazetta dei Leoncini.   98

15 THE CHILD CHRIST. Detail of the 10th-century mosaic uncovered in the south vestibule of Haghia Sophia. Christ the Child is shown as the Holy Wisdom, the Word of God.   99

16 THE IMPERIAL HOMAGE. The Emperor Leo VI the Wise adoring Christ the Divine Wisdom in a late-9th-century mosaic uncovered in the narthex of Haghia Sophia.   114

17 LINE AND TEXTURE. This Constantinopolitan goblet of the Macedonian period is now in the Treasury of San Marco at Venice. It has been chosen to represent through its simplicity the closest Byzantine approach to the court art of the early Sung emperors in China.   115

18 THE CHARACTER OF THE MACEDONIAN RENAISSANCE. An enamelled glass bowl in the Treasury of San Marco. This bowl of dark red glass enamelled in white, grey, green, red and lilac is most probably of the late 10th or early 11th century. It is typically Late Macedonian in its colour scheme, in the classical sources for its figure-work, in the rosettes and marks and in the Islamic influence apparent in the use of pseudo-Kufic script as a decoration of the inner rim.   130

Illustrations

19   THE ARCHANGEL MICHAEL. This is Constantino-   131
politan and late 10th century, and is now a part of
the Pala d'Oro behind the high altar in San Marco.
The Pala d'Oro ('The Golden Pall') is a composite of
enamels, beaten gold and jewels first commissioned
at Constantinople in 976, remodelled between 1102
and 1117, added to in the late 12th and 13th centuries
and framed in 1345. This plaque is one of its earliest
sections.

20   THE YOUNGER ALEXIOS COMNENOS. This mosaic   138
uncovered in the south gallery of Haghia Sophia is a
portrait of Alexios the eldest son of the Emperor
John II Comnenos. It has been dated as 1122.

21   THE CHRIST OF MONREALE. The late-12th-century   139
Christ in the apse of the cathedral of Monreale above
Palermo is almost as certainly Constantinopolitan as
the Virgin of Torcello (Plate 3) and perhaps represents
geometric tendencies as developed at the Capital
during a generation.

22   THE CRUCIFIXION. An enamel from the Pala d'Oro   146
(*see* Plate 19), most probably of the late 12th century.
The emphasis on emotional intensity and on the details
of the Passion scene are derived from the traditions of
provincial monastic art.

23   THE RAISING OF LAZARUS. A 15th-century wall-   147
painting in the church of the Pantanassa at Mistra.
The two masters of the Peribleptos and the three
masters of the Pantanassa form two groups, perhaps
two schools. The Raising of Lazarus is characteristic
of the Pantanassa masters in the strong modelling of
the forms and in the dramatic tension conveyed through
sudden action.

Illustrations

24   THE NATIVITY. Detail from a late-14th-century wall-   154
      painting in the church of the Peribleptos at Mistra
      above Sparta.

25   THE VIRGIN BENEATH THE CROSS. Detail of a   155
      panel-painting from Thessalonika of the late 14th or
      early 15th century. It is now in the Byzantine Museum
      at Athens.

Sources of Illustrations

The following sources of photographs are gratefully
acknowledged: 1, Fine Art Engravers Ltd; 2, 15, 18, 20,
Byzantine Institute Inc.; 3, 4, 5, 7, 12, 14, 17, 19, 22,
Mansell-Alinari; 6, 13, 21, 24, Cecil Stewart (from *Byzantine
Legacy*, published by George Allen and Unwin Ltd); 8,
Ediciones Mas, Barcelona; 9, Nicholas Young; 10, Musée
du Louvre; 11, Hermitage Museum; 16, Osvaldo Böhm;
25, Byzantine Museum, Athens. (Prints for 8, 10, 11, 16
lent by Phaidon Press Ltd and John Beckwith.)

Foreword

THIS BOOK WAS FIRST SUGGESTED TO ME BY PROFESSOR Thomas Whittemore, and in its initial stage owed much to the encouragement of M. Gabriel Millet.

I should express my gratitude for the facilities that have been given me by M. Soteriou and his colleagues at the Byzantine Museum at Athens; by Dr Paul Underwood and his colleagues at the Church of the Chora at Constantinople and at Haghia Sophia; by Mlle Antoniadis at the Byzantine Institute at Venice, and also to the Curator of the Treasury at San Marco; to the Directors of the Tretiakov Gallery and the Central Restoration Workshop at Moscow; and to members of the staff of the Louvre and the Musée Guimet, the Fitzwilliam Museum, the British Museum and the Victoria and Albert.

I would wish to acknowledge the hospitality I have received from the Communities of Vatopedi on Mount Athos, of St John on Patmos, and of St Katherine on Mount Sinai, and of Hosios Loukas and of the Pantanassa at Mistra.

I am grateful to all who have supplied my illustrations but would like to express particular thanks to Prof. Thomas Whittemore and Dr Paul Underwood; to Mr Cecil Stewart; to Mr John Beckwith and Phaidon Press Ltd, his publishers; to Sir Maurice Bowra; and finally to Messrs Faber and Faber Ltd, for allowing me to re-use the colour blocks of St John on Patmos whose preparation they supervised with such patience and care for my *Byzantine Painting*, published in their Faber Gallery in 1950.

But above all I am grateful for the suggestions that have been made to me by my personal friends, Ernest Barker, Norman Baynes, John Beckwith, Maurice Bowra, Georgina and William Buckler, Nicolete and Basil Gray, George Huxley, Christian

Foreword

Lucas, John Mavrogordato, Dmitri Obolensky, Emmy and Egon Wellesz, and Thomas Whittemore.

G. M.

Byzantine Aesthetics

BYZANTINE ART CAN ONLY BECOME INTELLIGIBLE WHEN considered in relation to the civilization of which it is an expression. The conservative element both in that civilization and in that art has been greatly over-estimated. Byzantine civilization may be considered in six distinct phases, and constant changes in taste, fashion and technique brought so many variations in art-forms that it is gradually becoming possible to date any Byzantine work with some exactness. Yet like Byzantine civilization Byzantine art possessed an overall unity. This is perhaps due to a continuity of its aesthetic standards.

Any approach to Byzantine aesthetics should take four factors into account: a recurrent taste for classical reminiscence, which expressed a conscious inheritance of a Graeco-Roman past; an essentially mathematical approach to beauty, which led to an emphasis not only on exact symmetry but on *eurhythmos* and balanced movements; an absorbed interest in optics, which led not only to many experiments in perspective but to a concentration on Light—conceived as in itself incorporeal, though finding expression in contrasted colours; and finally a belief in the existence of an invisible world of which the material is the shadow—so that an image presupposes the Imaged just as a shadow presupposes the human body that casts it, and is as closely linked to it. A scene is not a mere representation of something that has once happened but a *mimesis*, a re-enactment.

All Byzantine history and culture is derived from the crucial fact that the Roman Empire survived in unbroken continuity in the predominantly Greek-speaking provinces of the East, while the West sank into anarchy. The Byzantine ruler remained the Roman Emperor, his subjects conceived themselves as *Romaioi*, and even the medieval Byzantines were the conscious inheritors of an Hellenic tradition frozen and formalized. In her *Alexiad* Anna Comnena describes in a conflict with the Normans how 'the Caesar's bow was indeed the very bow of Apollo and he did not after the manner of the Homeric Greeks draw the string, but like a second Herakles'; and again 'the Queen stayed in the palace, for she was anxious about the fair-haired Menelaus as the poet says'. Knowledge of the classics was highly prized among both men and women. In the 12th century the Empress Irene could compose a commentary upon the *Iliad*; her sister-in-law Anna Comnena could state 'I perused the works of Aristotle and the dialogues of Plato'; and the author of a religious drama could begin, 'Now in the fashion of Euripides I tell the Passion that has saved the world.'

Classical art-forms must have retained prestige through their association with the literary classics and with the decorous pursuit of polite philosophy and good letters. They would have been primarily familiar through the classical statuary which still ornamented the Capital. Since sculpture was no longer practised in the round an attempt at exact reproduction of statuary was impossible, but this may explain why in Byzantine painting the conventional tendency was to render such classical reminiscences monumentally.

Yet though in any study of Byzantine aesthetics it is important to stress the recurrent nostalgia for the antique this was only one factor behind Byzantine art standards. Byzantine civilization had evolved from Graeco-Roman civilization but it had evolved very far; a Byzantine emperor was the legitimate successor of Hadrian, but there was a contrast between the luxurious informal intimacies of the villa at Tibur and the ballet-like Imperial liturgy of court ceremonial at Constantinople. The setting of the Byzantine palace was marked by that serene

2   THE CONQUEST OF DEATH
[*pp. 4, 10, 17, 39, 140*]

3   THE VIRGIN OF TORCELLO

[pp. 10, 35]

Byzantine zest for a nature frozen and transmuted, the small rooms with their walls half-covered with mosaic, the floors strewn with rosemary and myrtle, the golden pineapples, and the enamelled birds in the trees of gilded bronze. Life had moved on to a different plane from that at Tibur and the apt citations from Homer must have sounded strangely among the décor of the Byzantine court—the blue silk robes tight-girdled, the scented tapering beards, the harsh cosmetic and the great officials holding in their hands the red enamelled apples of their rank.

An interest in the natural properties of jewels, of herbs and of the planets was combined with lucid speculation upon ethics; ethics being conceived as the laws that govern human action and give purpose and therefore structure to a society. Both pre-supposed a conception of the intelligibility of nature, a conviction of the causality of law and a world view of hierarchic grades; Byzantine civilization was essentially mathematical in its emphasis on the inevitability of due proportion, rhythm and order. This sense of the inevitable reflected the underlying serenity of the self-concentrated Byzantine culture, based on recognition of the dominance of Idea and of the rule of cool and temperate mind.

From the 6th century, secular studies culminated in the *quadrivium* of arithmetic, astronomy, geometry and music. Of these it was geometry that possessed most prestige and perhaps gave deepest pleasure. The tenth chapter of the ninth book of the *Alexiad* contains the story of Nikephoros Diogenes. He had been blinded by the Emperor; 'thereupon he underwent a complete education and even most wonderful of all in far-famed geometry, and meeting one of the learned men he ordered him to furnish the figures to him in solid form. Then by the touch of hands he had apprehension of all the theorems and figures of geometry.'

Already in the 6th century Agathias described architecture

as the inventions of engineers who applied geometry to solid matter.[1] In the medieval Byzantine period constantly altering geometric patterns seem to underlie experiments in colouring.[2] Already much Byzantine painting can be expressed in terms of the varying proportion of rectangle to triangle and of intersecting semicircles.

This mathematical approach to beauty had of course its classic origins; Aristotle in the *Poetics* had stated that beauty consists in size and order, and Plato had already noted in the *Timaeus* that beauty is not without measure. But it may be suggested tentatively that the Byzantine approach was geometric rather than arithmetical. The primary aesthetic aim became the attempt to portray the inevitable development of exactly proportioned movement. At Constantinople this can be equally illustrated from the architecture of Haghia Sophia in the 6th century and from the paintings in the Chora church in the 14th. An appreciation of Russian ballet is still perhaps the best introduction to Byzantine aesthetics.

It will be suggested in the next chapter that such a conception had been foreshadowed during a 3rd-century transition in art; thus in the sixth *Ennead* of Plotinus, material beauty is described as symmetry irradiated by life. Symmetry of movement and in movement was contrasted with the symmetry that was dead. Some of this is conveyed by the description of the beauty of the Empress Irene Dukas in that very characteristic Byzantine document the *Alexiad*; she was: 'truly a breathing statue of beauty and a living monument of symmetry. For the most part her hand acted as a charioteer for her speech, in perfect harmony bringing forward the wrist with the arm, and you would have said that ivory had been carved by some craftsman into a framing of fingers and hands. Furthermore the iris of her eyes resembled a calm sea radiating forth its blue in deep waves of serenity, and the white of her eyes all round shone in rivalry of the iris and flushed forth irresistible grace and gave unspeakable charm to her glances.'[3]

As this passage suggests, there is a recurring Byzantine association between Life and Light and between light and the immaterial element in material things. Colour is conceived as light materialized. In Byzantine poetry natural colours are transcribed meticulously—as in the verse by John Geometres on the spring: 'the gracious gold-flowered crocus, the anemone, the narcissus gleaming whiter than the snow'. In Byzantine painting and mosaic there is often no relation between the colour combination chosen and the natural tint. Changing colour schemes are conceived in terms of rhythm. Perhaps both painting and mosaic were in some fashion apprehended as music and the colour combinations seen as harmony.

The emphasis on light and colour gave a particular significance to optical theory and experiment; in Haghia Sophia, at Hosios Loukas and at Daphni there are optical devices to increase the quantity of light within the mosaic. But optics were especially used to eliminate or redirect the effects of space. In the 5th century Proclus in his *Euclid* had defined *skenographia* as 'the practice which teaches the artist how to ensure that something in his work should not appear distorted by distance or height'. He repeated an earlier definition of perspective first phrased by Geminus: 'The laws which teach the monumental sculptor what his finished work will look like so that it will be eurhythmic to the eye of the beholder . . . works which are destined to be seen from a great distance do not appear as they really are.' This is one key to understanding Byzantine experiments in perspective, but a fuller consideration of the relations between Byzantine optics and geometry is better left to the chapter on the mathematical setting of Byzantine art.

One other factor should be allowed for in an introductory analysis of Byzantine surface-aesthetics. If the sense of rhythm and of colour variants was abnormally well developed among Byzantine connoisseurs this was perhaps even more true of the sense of touch. The study of Chinese porcelain is an admirable introduction to the study of Byzantine 'minor arts', which probably depended for much of their appeal on tactile sensation. Graeco-Roman civilization when it had moved at last onto the Byzantine plane acquired many of the characteristics of that of classical China.

Yet there was another form of Byzantine aesthetic apprehension besides that of surface-aesthetics. John Chrysostom had contrasted the two in the first of his Orations on the Incomprehensible in God: 'We admire many things; the beauty of a portico, of paintings, of a youthful body. We also admire the vastness of the Ocean; fear will be added to this admiration if we perceive the abyss of the depth of the sea, and it is this fear-admiration which the Psalmist experiences in contemplating the vast and immense Ocean of God's wisdom.'[4] This is perhaps reminiscent of Longinus on the Sublime, 'that echo that leads to ecstasy'.

Eastern Christianity made it possible for the Byzantine to experience both forms of aesthetic experience when contemplating a religious object. In terms of the Christianized Middle Platonism which underlies so much Byzantine theological speculation the first could be considered as the contemplation of beauty rendered visible, the second that of the beauty thus reflected.

Since the Alexandrian school of the 3rd century it had become a commonplace among Christian exegetes that the literal sense of Scripture, the letters and the numbers and the words, could contain a deeper hidden meaning. These mystic meanings could only be reached through concentration on each detail of the text, and the literal meaning was to the mystical as water is to wine. This provides the approach to the Byzantine use of symbolism in art. It is significant that this first appears in the creation of the symbols for the Great Mysterion, Baptism and Eucharist—Re-birth and New Life.

The whole liturgy developed from the ceremonies of Baptism and Eucharist. Initiation into the Mystery was an initiation into new transcendent life. All Byzantine religion centred round the performance of the *Leitourgia* conceived as a sacred drama; not a commemoration but a re-enactment. The infinity of Godhead taking flesh had given the Incarnation a reality that pierced through time and space.

Byzantine religious art was to become part of liturgy; on the walls of the sanctuary of San Vitale at Ravenna the sacrifice of the Eucharist is perpetually re-enacted in mosaic.

The conception of the sacred symbol and of forms of art that could be forms of liturgy preceded and perhaps also led to the use of images as objects of cult and to the custom of praying through the ikon to the Prototype it represented.

Byzantine art survived the final destruction of the Byzantine Empire when the Turks stormed Constantinople on the 29th of May in 1453 and the last of the Roman emperors, Constantine XI, died in the breach by the gate of St Romanos. Although Imperial patronage, which had been so crucial a factor in its development, vanished with the Byzantine court, the workshops in the Capital were not destroyed; but they were rapidly re-oriented to provide for the half-Persian tastes of the new rulers and then slowly transformed by the influx of Islamic craftsmen from such towns as Brusa. Monastic patronage stayed constant and was perhaps expanding; in the 16th century there was much rebuilding and fresh decoration in the abbeys on Athos and on Patmos. And there were still lay patrons of wealth in Crete, in Zante, in Corfu and among the Greek merchants at Venice.

The 16th-century Cretan school of Michael Damaskinos, to which El Greco seems first to have belonged, is at times in the pure Byzantine tradition. A considerable number of panels dating from perhaps 1480 to 1660 have recently been uncovered in the new workshop at Venice next to San Giorgio dei Greci; it is notable how many of these preserve the rhythms of earlier Byzantine painting and adhere exactly to its canons.

Still, the fact that so much of this work was being achieved within the sphere of Venetian influence or direct control made it susceptible to alien influences. The traditions of Byzantine painting slowly faded, weakened by the adoption of *Seicento* Italian mannerisms and by the strangely pervasive influence of Western woodcuts and engravings. Manuel Tzanes in his earlier work between 1655 and 1670 is perhaps the last Byzantine panel-painter. The last Byzantine wall-paintings are those by the monk John in the church of Kaisariani upon Hymettos; they are dated 1682.

The orthodox monastic art that succeeded the Byzantine perhaps came into being partly as a rigorist monastic reaction against early-17th-century 'Latin' mannerisms. It is very apparent as early as about 1640, it was exclusively dominant from about 1685 to 1870, and it survived into the 20th century as a peasant art, notably in Asia Minor. It is essentially the art of the ikon; the emphasis is on the single image not on the scene. Though much in it has been derived and distorted from Byzantine monastic sources, the Byzantine rhythms have vanished and the colour schemes that had been linked with them have altered.

Periodic over-paintings changed and deadened earlier Byzantine work both on church walls and on wooden panels.

It was a cardinal misfortune for the study of European art history that for so long what commonly passed as Byzantine painting was repainting or new painting from the late 17th to the middle of the 19th century and that 18th-century manuals like Denis of Fourna's *Painter's Guide* were assumed to represent immemorial practice. So many of the generalizations on 'the Byzantine' that are still on occasion current are in reality only applicable to the stiff, unchanging conventions of this formalized religious art.

Such a travesty of Byzantine art history is intelligible enough. In the first place it fitted admirably with the travesty of Byzantine cultural history which had evolved in the West in the 18th-century age of Enlightenment and which had been given its classic English form by Edward Gibbon. Again, much of the 19th-century research into art history was concentrated on Italian painting and there are superficial resemblances between the 18th-century Greek art of the ikon and the so-called *scuola Bizantina* which was held to precede Giotto. In fact the oddly styled *arte Bizantina* which the school of Giotto slowly ousted seems to have been old-fashioned and formalized provincial Italian, while it now seems increasingly likely that Giotto and Duccio were influenced by art movements in contemporary Constantinople.

But though this misconception of Byzantine art was intelligible it was not really excusable. Throughout the period when it was most widely current the 5th- and 6th-century mosaics at Ravenna were admired and studied and on occasion shockingly restored, and these cannot have been held to have supported its generalizations; nor could two easily accessible 12th-century Byzantine masterpieces—the Christ in the apse of

Cefalu and the Virgin in the apse of Torcello; nor could the 14th- and 15th-century wall-paintings in the churches of the Pantanassa and the Peribleptos at Mistra above Sparta. Yet it should be noted that all these are only isolated fragments of a great art that lasted over a thousand years.

There is no scholar to whom the history of Byzantine art owes more than to M. Millet. His study of the Mistra paintings was a prelude to a new epoch. But only the flood of new discoveries—beginning in 1935 with Professor Whittemore's work in Haghia Sophia—is at last making it possible to reconstruct the continuous history of Byzantine art and to attempt to analyse the aesthetic standards that it presupposes.

In Constantinople the mosaics in Haghia Sophia are still being slowly stripped of the Swiss and Turkish plaster-work that cover them. In the church of the Chora near the Adrianople Gate Dr Paul Underwood and his colleagues by revealing the mosaic cycles and discovering the great painting of the Anastasis have made the most important single contribution to the recovery of Byzantine art. The discovery of the mosaics in the Fetije Camii, of the wall-paintings in the buried church of St Euphemia, and of Byzantine decorated floorings, have not the same significance but they have suggested something of the developments in the Capital. Dr Talbot Rice's uncovering of the great floor mosaics in what is apparently the Palace Complex have illustrated vividly the classical roots of so much Byzantine court art.

Outside the Capital there has been a great accession to knowledge of the art of Salonika and of South Macedonia. The uncovering of the wall-paintings in the churches at Trebizond is providing fresh evidence for Byzantine colour aesthetics. The discoveries of M. Soteriou and his pupils have enabled us to reconstruct the developments of Byzantine art in Greece.

Byzantine masterpieces are also being found scattered along

the fringes of the Empire. On the most likely hypotheses the great paintings discovered at Castelseprio were the work of some 10th-century Byzantine artist employed by a Lombard prince, and the complicated and beautiful patterns of the floor mosaic discovered at the cathedral of Sabratha were sent to Tripolitania from Constantinople as a gift from the Emperor Justinian. Perhaps most important of all will be the analysis of the vast cache of Byzantine treasures preserved in the monastery of St Katherine on Mount Sinai, but this analysis is only in its early stages.

All this has been accompanied by a new scientific study of what have been so clumsily styled Byzantine 'minor arts': textiles, metalwork and enamels, goblets and carved ivories. In Byzantine civilization these arts are never 'minor'. Many of these new discoveries are by any standard masterpieces. In this book I shall study what may have made them masterpieces to the Byzantines.

2

The Third-Century Transition

ON THE 11TH OF MAY, 330, CONSTANTINE ESTABLISHED the administrative centre of the Roman Empire in the old Greek town of Byzantium, shortly to be renamed Constantinople. But Byzantine art was already coming into existence. During the 3rd century a change in content in classic art-forms and the creation of a Christian art that conveyed a hidden sacred meaning provided the frame for the development of Byzantine aesthetics —that is, for the Byzantine apprehension of beauty through sensual perception, *aisthesis*.

The acute phase of transition from classical to Byzantine culture occurred before Byzantium became a capital or Christianity a State religion. The confused and tangled epoch between the accession of Septimius Severus in 193 and the accession of Diocletian in 284 foreshadowed and shaped the future. Much that had marked the 2nd-century civilization of the Antonines—the sense of *gravitas* and the restraint of form; the tranquil acceptance of the interplay of individual privilege and obligation within a social structure conceived as effortlessly stable; the solid *bourgeois* standard of what was perhaps essentially a small-town culture—went down in the chaos of an economic collapse. There was a re-orientation and reorganization both of economic life and of the State which was to survive under slightly varying forms until the destruction of the Byzantine Empire. This synchronized with the temporary triumph of the cult of the Unconquered Sun and the emergence of Neo-Platonism, as much a religion as it was a philosophy. It is tenable that the turning-point in Mediterranean religious experience was the 3rd-century victory of transcendent monotheism rather than the 4th-century conversion to Christianity which was its sequel.

Constantine was the disciple of the *Summus Deus* before he became the patron of the Christians.

New conventions in Imperial portraiture seem to symbolize a change in the conception of the functions of personality and of sovereignty and of the relationship of man with the Divine and of man with men. All art-forms shift and alter in this period, and it is also possible to trace a new content in the old literary conventions. The extent to which these changes were inter-connected and governed by a single rhythm is difficult to decide, but the fact of a 3rd-century transition is patent and the period between 253 and 268 remains one of its most significant episodes. Both in art and in philosophy its standards seem to form a bridge between the classic and Byzantine worlds.

The 3rd-century changes within the Graeco-Roman worlds were not continuous. This was due to the coexistence of distinct cultural traditions, differentiated less by the nature of their ingredients than by their proportion; to the economic survival of great vested interests like that of the central Senatorial grouping; and to the wide acceptance of the inevitability of classical standards of value. Three strands in the 3rd-century transition are distinct though interwoven. It is possible to trace one line of development from the Emperor Decius through Aurelian to Diocletian so that the years 249–51, 270–5, 284–305 may be studied as a single unit. It is possible to trace a tradition perpetuated in a Senatorial milieu and represented by the three Gordian emperors, by Pupienus and Balbinus, Tacitus and Florian, and perhaps to some extent by Claudius II and Quintillus, so that the years 238–44, 268–70, 275–6 have a certain similarity. Again there are clearly links between 222–35, 253–68, 276–82, the principates of Severus Alexander, Gallienus and Probus; this is the line which leads to Constantine in 306. In each grouping some unity is apparent, not only in State policy and in the official propaganda of the coins, but in art-forms; of the three, that which centred round Gallienus has the most significance for the official future. Constantine was far more truly the successor of Gallienus than he was of Diocletian. It is therefore worth analysing in some detail the art-forms of the Gallienic phase, 253–68.

The Emperor Gallienus seems linked with a grouping who were to maintain for five more generations many of the traditions of the Antonines. He was consciously classical in his inspiration and had Augustus and Hadrian as his models. His wife Salonina seems the last of that line of Imperial women who derive from Livia, and the qualities ascribed to her at the Roman mint are the traditional ideals *pudicitia* and *fecunditas*. His gold medallions for his son Saloninus, *Principi Iuventutis*, intentionally suggest the same Augustan flavour. But there is the coming of a new note in the *Virtus Augusti* series on his coinage: he is Hercules, and the endurance and the tasks of Hercules combine to form the imperial *virtus*; he is Mercury, messenger from the gods to men; he is the genius of Rome distinct from and re-entering his city.[1] All this, taken in conjunction with the upward glance—which first appears with him in Imperial portraiture and which was to become so characteristic of the self-representations of Constantine—seems to convey a new conception of Imperial power. No longer strong through an immanent divinity, this power reflects by divine right another and transcendent godhead; it forms a link between two coexisting worlds yet remains isolated by very reason of that function. Here is the Byzantine concept of sovereignty.

Yet the changes that are foreshadowed are not the changes that are foreseen. The true emotional background of that time is perhaps best suggested by the bulk of the coin inscriptions from the Imperial mints between 260 and 268: *Securitas Perpetuitus, Ubique Pax, Securitas Perpetua, Securitas Publica, Securitas*

Orbis, Aeternitati Augusti, Felicitas Aeterna, ob Conservationem Salutis, Restitutor Orbis, Pacator, Conservator. A new world came slowly into being through an attempt to preserve the old, for the art movement that centres in those eight years seems marked by a straining effort to retain the stability, the world view and the standards of the Hadrianic Age. Gallienus was a patron of this movement but his patronage was not its cause; it is equally apparent at the mints under the control of his rival Postumus and on Gallic sarcophagi. As a movement it was to be ultimately frustrated because the Hadrianic world view presupposed a world order which was no longer economically viable. Even during those eight years the arbitrary value attached by the Imperial authority to the new inflation currency and the attempt of the Government to enforce the acceptance of the new issue at the official rate imply the end of the free interplay of economic forces which had done so much to create 2nd-century culture. The passionate emphasis on stability marked a *bourgeoisie* in process of being liquidated.

Gallienic art-forms achieved parallels with those of Hadrianic art; they remain Graeco-Roman and unorientalized. The change is in content. The bust of Gallienus in the Louvre is clearly Augustan in inspiration; the bust of Gallienus in the Museo delle Terme is modelled on Hellenistic Late Antonine; but in both there is an essentially romantic rendering of life in transience which has no known 1st- or 2nd-century source. In 3rd-century bust-portraiture there is already present the Byzantine effort to discern and to convey the spirit, the *pneuma* that is enshrouded in the flesh. Imperial Hellenistic art is moving perhaps unconsciously onto a fresh plane of expression.

The new type of the philosopher-sage on the sarcophagi is, in desire at least, an aesthetic reaction. It can be associated with the Postumus coin-type from the Lyons mint. It is marked by a nostalgia for tranquillity and restraint and for an artificial Hellenism: for all, in fact, that a generation earlier might have seemed to be going out of fashion, whether through the emotionalism of the Ludovisi sarcophagus or through the tortured strength of the bust of the Emperor Philip. Yet from it there derives in unbroken continuity the austere conception of an eternal priesthood that forms the Byzantine convention of an Evangelist's or of a Bishop's portrait.[2] On the Philosopher sarcophagus of the Lateran the grouping of the Sage and his disciples foreshadows a Byzantine Christ and His Apostles, while the new form of centralized composition is a technical innovation which led to the 10th-century mosaic in the narthex of Haghia Sophia. There the Emperor Leo the Wise crouches, adoring Christ as Light, in the presence of the Virgin and of the Genius of the City.

Again this phase is marked by a crucial transition in the practice of allegory in art—from an attribute represented as embodied, to a human individual represented as an embodied attribute. The initiation of Gallienus in the Mysteries at Eleusis was in itself an attempt to return to Hadrianic Hellenism. Its commemoration results in the coin-type *Galliena Augusta*, with the Emperor as the goddess Demeter, Majesty depersonalized and desexed, a foreshadowing of that long line of Byzantine Imperial portraiture in which the subject is less the individual than Majesty irradiated by the Divine. The wide variations in the portrayal of the Emperor seem intended like his *Virtus Augusti* series to emphasize the functions of his office and the distinction between his rôles ; there is a Gallienus as the god Serapis, as Alexander, as the source of new fertility and as the saviour of his people.

But the classicist trend in the art of the late 3rd century gained its meaning from an unimaginable future, not from a half-imagined past. The silver disk of Parabiago now in the Brera Gallery at Milan seems to belong either to the period of Gallienus or perhaps more probably to that of Constantine. The subject is Cybele and the Seasons, the world scheme that it sets out to portray is the closed classic world, but there is a new romantic rendering of life in movement and its dancing rhythm foreshadows that of the 14th-century painting in the church of the Chora at Constantinople where Christ triumphs over Death.

The late 3rd century also coincided with a new development in aesthetic theory. This may have been closely associated with the character of Gallienic classicism, for some phrases from Porphyry[3] suggest its immediate setting: 'From about the first year of Gallienus, Plotinus had begun to write upon such subjects as had arisen in his lectures. When I first came to know him in the tenth year of the reign he had composed twenty-one treatises. . . . The Emperor Gallienus and his wife greatly honoured and venerated him.'

The only conscious innovation in the ideals of Gallienic art-forms would seem to be a new emphasis on life in movement seen in relation to an eternal attribute. Plotinus wrote in the sixth *Ennead*:[4] 'We have to recognize that beauty is that which irradiates symmetry rather than symmetry itself, and it is that which truly calls out love. Why else is there more of the glory of beauty upon the living and only some faint traces of it upon the dead, even though the face still retains its fullness and symmetry? Why are the most living portraits the most beautiful?'

This is in contrast to the conventional classical aesthetic by which beauty consists only in proportion of parts and harmony of colour. Plotinus wrote in the first *Ennead*:[5] 'Almost everyone declares that the symmetry of parts towards each other and to-wards a whole, with besides a certain charm of colour, con-stitutes the beauty recognized by the eye; that in visible things, as indeed in all else universally, the beautiful thing is essentially symmetrical and patterned.'

Embodied life is in motion because it is embodied—the symmetrical corpse is motionless because lifeless. The living, moving body is more beautiful and real than the corpse because it is linked with an eternal attribute; its beauty is derived from the incorporeal and therefore immutable Beauty that is God. This could be applied to the representations in art of live or of dead symmetry.

Again a corpse is matter in process of disintegration, a live body is beautiful because of its unity. So too in art, symmetry or rhythm are not beautiful because of the diversity of their parts but because of the essential unity that the very diversity conveys. In art the giving of that unity is an act of mind. 'The form is not in the material, it is in the designer before ever it enters into the stone.'[6] 'On what principle does the architect when he finds the house standing before him correspondent with his inner ideal of the house pronounce it beautiful? Is it not that the house before him, the stones apart, is the inner idea stamped upon the mass of exterior matter, the indivisible exhibited in diversity?'[7]

This brought with it a new conception of the function of the artist as creator. 'The arts give no bare reproduction of the thing seen, but go back to the ideas from which nature itself derives, and furthermore much of their work is all their own; they are holders of beauty and add where nature is lacking. Thus Pheidias wrought Zeus upon no model among things of sense, but by apprehending what form Zeus must take if he chose to become manifest to sight.'[8]

'Where the ideal form has entered it has grouped and co-ordinated what from a diversity of parts was to become a unity, it has rallied confusion into co-operation, it has made the sum one harmonious coherence . . . on what has thus been com-

4 THE DANCE OF CYBELE AND THE SEASONS
[*p. 17*]

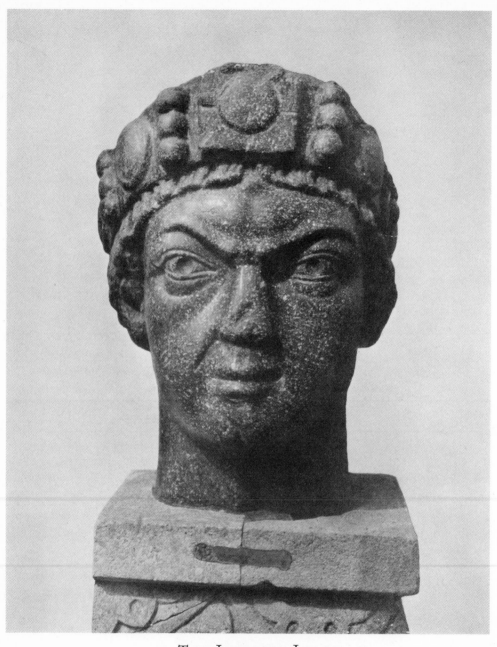

5   THE IMPERIAL IMAGE
[*p. 13*]

pacted into unity. Beauty enthrones itself, giving itself to the parts as to the sum . . . this then is how the material thing becomes beautiful—by communicating in the thought that flows from the Divine.'[9]

This was a conception in aesthetics that brought new freedom to the craftsman. Byzantine painters were to style themselves the *zoographoi*, the depictors of the living, but they were never to show that impelling desire to reproduce what the eye perceives which is the mark of antique illusionist painting.

Again, the Neo-Platonist theory of knowledge with its emphasis on contemplation and on the supremacy of the contemplative act in human thought brought with it a theory of aesthetic experience. Beauty is perceived aesthetically, that is by *aisthesis*, the power of sensual perception; either by the sight or —in the case of music and poetry—by hearing. It is not reached by analytic or discursive reason but is apprehended by a sudden vision. In art the perception of unity is an act of mind. The aesthetics of Plotinus provide the formulae which render all periods of Byzantine art intelligible. M. André Grabar has suggested that they contain the Byzantine techniques of the suppression of space dimensions for the dematerialization of reality; the foreshortening of figures; reversed perspective; and the use of the horizon line.[10]

The characteristic Byzantine conception of the relation between colour and light, and the Byzantine delight in the colour of gold, are already explicit in the first *Ennead*. 'All the loveliness of colour and the light of the sun.'[11] 'And how comes gold to be a beautiful thing? And lightning by night and stars, why are these so fair?'[12]

'The beauty of colour is also the outcome of unification; it derives from shape, from the conquest of the darkness inherent in matter by the pouring in of light, the unembodied.'

.

'Fire itself is splendid beyond all material bodies . . . it has colour primally, they receive the Form of colour from it: hence the splendour of its light . . . and all that has resisted and is but uncertainly held by its light remains outside of beauty as not having absorbed the plenitude of the Form of colour.'[13] 'Material forms containing light incorporated in them need still a light apart from them that their own light may be made manifest.'[14]

Yet there is little literary evidence that the *Enneads* were known to the Byzantines; the few references to Plotinus could be drawn from some late classical anthology. The Platonism that became an integral part in so much Byzantine thought was the old-fashioned Stoicized Middle Platonism that Basil of Caesarea and Gregory Nazianzen had been taught in Athens; that which Gregory of Nyssa had chosen as the framework for his own speculation. The Neo-Platonism that the Byzantines knew was essentially that formulated in the 5th century by Proclus,[15] and this though sporadically influential was also suspect. All that can be stated with certainty is that the altering art-forms of the late 3rd century coincided with the creation of a new Greek theory of aesthetics which provides an explanation for much of Byzantine art.

As an analysis of the technical terminology of the sixth *Ennead* will suggest, Plotinus was as much influenced by the technique of classical philosophy as a contemporary Gallienic artist would have been by that of classical sculpture. It is possible to trace in both the same rejection of barbarian syncretisms; the *Enneads* belong very clearly to a different world from that of the *Hermetica*. It is not that with Plotinus Greek speculation is ceasing to be Greek; it is only moving onto another plane. 'Life here with the things of earth is a sinking, a defeat, a failing of the wing.' 'The soul of its nature loves God and longs to be at one with him.' 'There the soul is Aphrodite of the Heavens but here turned harlot, an Aphrodite of the Public Ways; but the soul is always Aphrodite.' 'The soul taking that outflow from the Divine is stirred, seized by a Bacchic passion; goaded by these goads, it becomes love.'

The background is Hellenist enough; there are the echoes from two myths and a source in the *Symposion*, but there is a new note in the essentially romantic passion for the Divine. This is an amalgam that is characteristically 3rd century.[16] In the *Aethiopica* the new high-wrought conception of virginity appears and reappears in those fantastic situations derived from the conventions of 1st- and 2nd-century rhetorical training. The *Banquet of the Twelve Virgins* by the Christian Methodios of Olympos dates from the close of the period. It is based on the *Symposion* as its central model; its introduction is a mosaic from the *Theaetetos* and the *Phaedros*; it ends with an echo from the *Republic* following on an echo from the *Hippolytos*. Yet it belongs to the new world in which embodied attributes mingle with individuals treated allegorically, and its motif lies in its repeated versicle: 'I keep myself pure for thee, O Bridegroom, and holding a lighted torch I go to meet thee. . . . I desire to gaze for ever on Thy Beauty.'[17]

The case could easily be overstated—the love and worship of God for His sake alone had already become rooted in Hellenistic tradition with the Stoics; the devotion is patent in the Cleanthes Hymn and sporadic in Epictetus—but in the *Enneads* the Stoic sense of worship has been charged with a new content, since worship now has its *raison d'être* in Otherness. For the Stoic the sense of worship is directed to an all-pervading immanent Divine force precisely because it is immanent. 'Shall we not say "Dear City of Zeus"?' But the Plotinian One is the object of desire precisely because transcendent. The object apprehended as transcendent 'is' so much beyond and above all others as 'to be' in quite a different sense from what they are. The transcendent conceived as the object of desire is the subject of all Byzantine mysticism. The object of desire conceived as if it were transcendent is the keynote to much of later romantic literature.

During the 3rd century, Graeco-Roman civilization was still in some sense a unit; the character of the transition in it would seem fundamentally one. It has been suggested above that the change may have been largely due to a suddenly chaotic social structure coincident with economic chaos. If the years 253 to 268 form its most illuminating phase it is precisely because an intentional conservatism throws the new elements into such relief. The new movements are equally apparent in thought and art and follow a parallel in both; conservative rather than revolutionary by design, and consciously based on classic models, they yet synchronize with and presuppose a new conception of world order. An emphasis on human life in transience and perhaps an experience of chaos had led to an overwhelming sense of the transcendent and immutable. This was to result in the Byzantine tradition of the de-individualization and stylization of the person by an eternal attribute. But it was also to include the twin motifs of the medieval romantic: the vision of an unique personal relationship which could transcend flux and time, and the vision of a human personality isolated in a world without horizon. That is why so often during the 3rd-century transition in both art and letters the classic mould seems suddenly to be broken by a new romantic tension. The religious instinct was coming to find expression through that form of other-worldliness in which the other world is conceived not merely as consecutive on this but primarily as coincident with it.[18]

3

The Mathematical Setting

SOME TIME BETWEEN 383 AND 390 ST GREGORY OF Nyssa in the *Catechetical Oration* gave the classic Byzantine form to the distinction between the world of mind and the material world.[1] This distinction between *noetos* and *aisthetos* had been derived directly from his Middle-Platonist masters. But the 3rd-century school of Alexandria had already prepared Greek Patristic thought for its reception and in the new Christian milieu it was to be both elaborated and clarified.

Like his friend St Gregory Nazianzen, St Gregory of Nyssa conceived Man as the bridge linking the two worlds in which all Being was divided. For them both a crucial text was Genesis 2. 7; God had formed Man from the dust of the earth and breathed into his nostrils the breath of life. By reason of his body man belongs to the world of matter; by reason of his soul he belongs to the world of mind. In man alone Mind and Matter, the worlds of *noetos* and *aisthetos*, intermingle and interpenetrate; through man alone the material becomes articulate in the praise of God: without him 'Mind and Sense remained distinct within their boundaries, bearing within themselves the Magnificence of the Creator Logos, but praising silently. . . . Nor was there any mingling between them; nor yet were the riches of God's goodness manifested . . . till Man was placed on earth as a kind of second world, a microcosm, a new angel, a mingled worshipper, . . . visible and yet intelligible, . . . to be the husbandman of immortal plants.'[2]

This is perhaps as close as we will ever get to the Byzantine conception of the essential function of all forms of religious art. Because Man is body he shares in the material world around him, which passes within him through his sense perceptions. Because

Man is Mind he belongs to the world of higher reality and pure spirit. Because he is both, he is in Cyril of Alexandria's phrase 'God's crowned image'; he can mould and manipulate the material and render it articulate. The sound in a Byzantine hymn, the gestures in a liturgy, the bricks in a church, the cubes in a mosaic are matter made articulate in the Divine praise. All become articulate through becoming part of a rhythm. In the world of matter they have become echoes of harmonies in the world of mind. This could explain the crucial importance of mathematics for Byzantine aesthetics.

For the Byzantine mathematician the theory of numbers and pure geometry belong to the wrold of *noetos*; the art of calculation, applied geometry, of optics and mechanics to that of *aisthetos*. Material was moulded inevitably by the laws of mind. It was perhaps precisely the note of inevitability which gave mathematical studies so great an appeal to the Byzantines. They seem to have been the only forms of study in which the desirability of innovation was admitted by the conventions of Byzantine education. Classical texts could be memorized, or explained, or chosen as models; no scholar would have admitted that they could be improved on. The creative period in East Christian theology ended in the 7th century; after that theologians as great as St John of Damascus, as accomplished as Euthymios Zigabenos, were content to synthesize and to expound the 'Axioms of the Fathers'—it does not seem to have been conceived possible that they should be added to. In the history of Byzantine philosophy it seems likely that much originality was disguised as commentary. But in applied mathematics innovations were to be claimed persistently, and at times unjustifiably, throughout the history of the Empire.[3] Perhaps this was partly because applied mathematics were conceived as mutable, since dealing with matter they formed part of the world of *aisthetos*. The same reason can also explain why technical innovations were admired in Byzantine architecture and art-forms.

There was never any place in the Byzantine social structure for the Western conception of the architect and of the artist. The normal anonymity of the Byzantine artist is due to his social obscurity; the signed ikons of the 16th and 17th centuries are the effect of the new status accorded to the painter in the Venetian sphere in Greece. There was a difference in conception between the artist as a craftsman, and the architect as an engineer. The engineer could be famous—Paulus Silentiarius wrote verses of pure panegyric on Anthemius for designing Haghia Sophia; but no one troubled to record the artisans who worked under his direction to embellish it.

Yet the architect and the artist were linked together in a web of mathematics. Clearly there were some provincial architects who were no more than unskilled builders and some provincial painters who were no more than untrained journeymen; but normally Byzantine architecture presupposes a knowledge of geometry and mechanics on the part of the architect, and Byzantine art normally presupposes some knowledge of optics, mensuration and simple geometry on the part of the artist. It is therefore worth classifying the forms of Byzantine mathematics and suggesting the relevance of each for the developments in Byzantine art.[4]

Byzantine mathematicians retained the fundamental distinction between arithmetic as the theory of number and logistic as the art of calculation—pure number applied to the material, to apples or sheep or bowls, or to the shares in some rich man's fortune. Arithmetic would seem to have been taught primarily by means of commentary. The most popular source for such commentaries was the *Isagoge* of Nicomachus of Gerasa. This has some significance for aesthetics, for Nicomachus was a

Neo-Pythagorean of the 1st century A.D., a theorist on music and intent on the harmonies as well as the mystic meanings of numbers.[5] He was commented on by Iamblichus in the 4th century;[6] in the 5th by Proclus, and in the 6th by Asclepios of Tralles and by John Philoponos of Alexandria.[7] As late as the early 14th century George Pachymeres used excerpts from Nicomachus for his introduction to arithmetic.

A Neo-Pythagorean emphasis on number as the ultimate reality blended with a system of scriptural exegesis already established by the 4th century. As Methodios had noted 'the entire creation of the world was achieved out of the harmony of the number six'.[8] Six also represented the process of the Incarnation; multiplied by ten it became the symbol of Christ. The harmony of six consists in the perfect harmony of its components; 'nothing in it is excessive or deficient'. 'When it is divided into equal parts by equal parts it must result in the same number again from its divided segments'; 'divided by three it becomes two, divided by two it becomes three, divided by six it becomes one'; 'when two and three and one are added it becomes six again'.[9] In the close study of any Byzantine work of art it is perhaps worth first looking for the proportion of three to two or of six to one. Byzantine 'surface-aesthetic' was inevitably derived from arithmetic since all harmonies in form or colour were the echoes of an incorporeal music, the harmonies of Pure Number.

Since logistics or the art of calculation was the means by which the theory of number was applied to material objects, facility in it was prized; it appealed to the Byzantine admiration for the quick-witted. Logistic epigrams became a section of the Byzantine Anthology. Forty-six are ascribed to Metrodoros, who lived in the reign of Justin I (518–527). The subjects chosen are material enough: how to divide a number of nuts, or to calculate the speed with which a pipe might be emptied or a vessel filled or a brickmaker produce his tally of bricks. The majority find their solution in forms of equation.

Inevitably logistics tended to blend with mechanics. Mechanics itself was primarily the art of the Byzantine builder but there were also two specialized branches *belopoeika* and *thaumatopoiike*. *Belopoeika*[10] dealt with the invention and the construction of engines of war—the variants of Greek Fire and the methods of throwing it, the attempts to blind assailants or to burn their ships through the use of mirrors, the development of siege implements. When added to mensuration it produced the Byzantine systems of fortifications which revolutionized those of Western Europe and of the Middle East.

Thaumatopoiike implied the craft of making wonders. It included the Imperial throne, forms of fountain and of organ, automatic machines and moving puppets. Neither *belopoeika* nor *thaumatopoiike* were concerned with art-forms, though many of the 'marvels' may have been works of art. But both must have stimulated the zest for ingenious contrivance.

Once again the late 3rd and the 4th century seem to be the formative period. The new utilitarian encyclopaedic approach to mechanics is first apparent in the writings of Heron of Alexandria with his treatises on the automaton theatre[11] and on water-clocks, his *pneumatika*[12] and his *belopoeika* and his *cheirobalistra*.[13] His most probable period is the late 3rd century A.D.; it has been suggested that the 'Most Illustrious' Dionysius who was his patron was the Prefect of the City in 301. But it is vital for any understanding of the Byzantine approach to mechanics that the 'cumulative' character of the Heron texts should be stressed. They could be added to, they had none of the sacrosanct quality of a text of a classic.[14]

Heron's place in Byzantine mechanics is paralleled in Byzantine geometry by that of his younger contemporary Pappus. The study of classical geometry had faded during the first centuries of the Roman Empire—according to one theory it had been in abeyance. Pappus compiled his *Synagoge*[15] as a deliberate attempt to revive it and in this he succeeded. Towards the end of the 4th century his work was completed by Theon of Alexandria, Hypatia's father. He is cited as an authority by Proclus. The great geometricians of the age of Justinian—Eutocius, Anthemius, Isidore—were his heirs. If the beauty of great Byzantine architecture is purely geometric, if there is a geometric element in the beauty of so much Byzantine art, both are largely due to Pappus of Alexandria.

Pure geometry and the theory of numbers were conceived as closely linked; in a Late Byzantine phrase they interpenetrated each other. The harmonies of number could be translated into geometric terms: a hundred as the circumference of a circle or six as an isosceles triangle. Though both belonged to the world of *noetos*, both moulded subordinate arts in *aisthetos* and the material world. It was this that led Michael Psellos in the 11th century to note the value of mathematics for philosophy since it linked abstract thought and material things.

The art of *geodaisia* was related to geometry as the art of calculation was to the theory of numbers. *Geodaisia* was the art of measurement of volume and surface. It was essentially practical. Proclus noted that it was not the function of geodesy to measure a cylinder as a cylinder but a pit as a cylinder, not a cone as a cone but a heap as a cone.[16] Because of this geodesy was treated experimentally; there is a 10th-century Geodesy, which is based on observations taken at the Hippodrome. About 1350 Isaac Argyros composed a *Method of Geodesy*. It seems never to have possessed the fashionable vogue of logistics, but some technical training in it is presupposed by the work of many Byzantine mosaicists. As Dr Otto Demus has noted 'middle Byzantine mosaic painting came to maturity and found its proper place on curved surfaces'.[17] Geodesy blended with optics. The careful placing of mosaic tessellae on squinches and pendentives, in cupolas and vaults was influenced by optical theory. Even on plain surfaces it became the custom to curve the setting bed in order to deflect the light. Although the deviations from the vertical and the undulations in surface measurement are commonly very slight they seem too carefully contrived to be anything except deliberate.

An example may be given from personal experience. There is evidence for three stages in the preparation of the mosaic of the Mother and Child in the vestibule of Haghia Sophia. A rendering bed of mixed lime and marble dust and a little sedge covers the uniform texture of the bricks to an average depth of 2.4 cm. This was keyed with indentations to receive a second bed of the same mixture averaging 1.5 cm thick. The setting bed of finer, whiter lime was placed above it in order to receive the mosaic cubes. But the setting bed is of varying thickness so that the mosaic is slightly curving even though the deviation from the vertical is only 5.5 cm. In contrast the gold and silver tessellae that form the background are set with their surfaces inclining forward while the gold and tawny tessellae that form the border are set vertically. The intricate measuring and angling of the mosaic are best explained if it was intended to be seen at thirteen metres from its centre at man's height from the floor. Geodesy was being used as an implement in optics.

The *Optics* of Euclid reached the Byzantine world through Pappus of Alexandria who had included it in his *Little Astronomy*. It remained current under two forms.[18] The longer version seems to have been the more used; it is a late-4th-century recension by Theon of Alexandria with a preface added by one of his disciples. But the shorter version in the *Little Astronomy* was copied and recopied[19] and extracts apparently from both are relatively common. The first four definitions are crucial for Byzantine theories of vision. 'Those things are seen on which the visual rays impinge while those are not seen on which they do not'; the process of vision is due to rays from the eyes striking against the objects. These rays are straight, 'the straight rays that issue from the eye traverse dimensions'. They create the field of vision by striking the object at an angle. 'The figure contained by the visual rays is a cone which has its vertex in the eye and its base at the extremities of the objects seen. . . . Things seen under a greater angle appear greater and those under a lesser angle less.' Since the visual rays are distinct and separate from each other a man can never see the whole of an object even though he believes that he is doing so (Proposition 1). Only by moving the eyes could all the surface be touched by the visual rays. The custom of gazing at a decorated surface is perhaps essentially Western. The *Ekphraseis*, Byzantine descriptions and panegyrics upon buildings, emphasize repeatedly that the eyes should not rest on decoration but should wander.[20]

It was this school in optics combined with *Catoptrica* which produced the Byzantine systems of perspective. Proclus considered *Catoptrica* to be a branch of optics. The primary sources in Byzantine mathematics were the *Catoptrica* attributed to Euclid,[21] almost certainly a compilation made about A.D. 400—and also a treatise by Heron.[22] Their conclusions were to be added to notably by Anthemius of Tralles.[23] Although Euclid's *Catoptrica* dealt primarily with the construction and combination of mirrors its significance for Byzantine aesthetics lay in its theory on angles of incidence and on the reflection and the refraction of light. For Proclus the third branch of optics was skenography, a term that covered all techniques in perspective, devices to regulate the effects of space between seer and seen as well as to link the fore-ground and background within the picture.

It was at one time maintained that Byzantine artists had no exact system of perspective. It is now becoming apparent that they had too many. Dr A. Michelis seems to have held an inter-mediate position. He wrote that 'the Byzantine artist although he followed no rational system of perspective had nevertheless a "knack" of seeing and representing this. Depth seemed to him not of the same value optically as width and height. The first plane was predominant.'[24] 'Knack' seems an inadequate phrase for deliberate and minutely planned contrivances. Depth was considered more important optically than width or height but it was conceived as being in front of the mosaic or picture, not behind it. In the Renaissance system of perspective the picture is conceived as a window opening on to a space beyond; it is the *pariete di vetro* of Leonardo da Vinci, the *fenestra aperta* of Leon Battista Alberti.[25] The Byzantine mosaic or picture opens onto the space before it. The 'picture space' of Byzantine art was primarily that of the church or palace room in which it was placed, since art was considered a functional part of architecture.

I have found no evidence for the often repeated statement that Byzantine culture had evolved a fresh theory of space, nor do I know of any literary support for the suggestion that a sense of infinite space was conveyed by the use of a gold background, though gold may partly have been chosen because of its associa-tion with light. Space as conceived by the Byzantine architect or artist seems always to have been Euclidean space measured by depth, height and width. If a Byzantine artist is primarily con-cerned with height and width it is because it is his primary task to provide surface decoration for floor or for ceiling or for wall.

Had the conventions of Byzantine art been restricted to the Image and to the Symbol it might well have become purely two-dimensional and its perspective contrivances would have been limited to the attempts to calculate, and at times to counteract, the effects of distance on the Euclidean visual rays. But there was also a tradition of representing scenes of action as surface decoration, which is already very notable in 4th- and 5th-century floor mosaics. As such scenes tended to grow more dramatic they also grew more crowded, and it became imperative to utilize or evolve contrivances which would give some form of depth within the mosaic itself. Hellenistic illusionist painting provided a quarry for such techniques and it was always a potential influence in Byzantium through its survival in manuscript illuminations. No Byzantine picture or mosaic ever became a window. Some of them became niches, knocked in a wall with their own box-like picture space, their own depth as well as height and breadth. It was this Byzantine fashion for the representation of 'box space' which provided the *stil nuovo* for Giotto. His paintings in the Arena are paralleled by the contemporary mosaics which have only recently been completely uncovered in the Kahrie Camii. Historically it is more probable that the common source for both was provided by Constantinople rather than by Padua. The window-perspective of the Italian High Renaissance was to develop from the box-space perspective of Giotto.

One characteristically Byzantine device for conveying depth in picture space was that of inverted perspective. The viewpoint of the picture is behind the scene not in front of it, and figures are shown smaller in proportion to their distance from the viewpoint. Dr A. Grabar has shown that this theory of perspective is consonant with Neo-Platonist theories of vision,[26] but it would also seem reasonable enough to a craftsman who had never heard of Plotinus or Proclus and had only a secondhand oral knowledge of the first definitions in Euclid's *Optics*. If the visual rays were to pass from the object to the eye it would be natural for the impression conveyed to be like that of a seal on wax, but if as the *Optics* asserted they passed from the eyes to the object it would be natural for the object to be shown as it exists in itself. The viewpoint could also be higher than the scene; so that the proportions of the scene or building would be visualized as they would appear from above, on occasion with a diminishing perspective. At times both contrivances would be combined and the viewpoint be placed both behind and above, as in the 5th-century mosaic in the church of St George at Salonika.

There were other technical contrivances. There was another form of aerial perspective defined as 'the use of colour to give the illusion of spatial coherence'; the Hellenistic motif of jagged rocks was inserted to divide foreground and background; there was the use of what has been called 'the flat axial system of parallel planes' and defined as 'the use of the same surface to carry dimensions which are perceived in succession by several acts of seeing'; there was the juxtaposition of curved and flat, angular and flat grounds; and there was the use of the terrace or of the slope.

Yet it should be stressed that all such contrivances are relatively rare in Early and Middle Byzantine art. During the 10th, 11th and early 12th centuries they survived primarily in manuscript illumination. It is only during the late 12th, the 13th, 14th, and early 15th centuries, that the representation of functional space became a dominant concern of Byzantine artists both in panel- and wall-paintings and in mosaics.

This led to an evolution in spatial composition. Figures in three-quarter view are oblique to the picture plane and related to the architectural niches that open onto that plane at an angle of forty-five degrees. New colour rhythms strengthen and accentuate the structure of the composition. Increasingly the horizon line is placed high. Perspective elements tend to converge downwards from top to bottom instead of receding—as in one Western fashion—from foreground into background. At times the co-existence of two surfaces and even of two spaces within one composition is conveyed by a counterpoint of geometrical elements and emphasized by tonal values in colour chosen without relation to any natural colouring.

This will be discussed more fully in the chapter on art standards under the Palaeologoi. But here it should be noted that none of these Palaeologan developments were revolutionary. They evolved directly from techniques in Hellenistic illusionist painting combined with experiments in colour already traceable in the 5th and 6th centuries. They presupposed traditional mathematics. It is a useful practice to attempt to reconstruct the dissective lines when studying 14th-century mosaic or painting. To the end Byzantine art was also a form of applied geometry.

Even in the last Byzantine period the primary function of skenography would seem to have remained that formulated by Geminus of Rhodes in the last century before Christ—a study of those laws which teach the artist what his finished work will look like so that it will be 'eurhythmic to the eye of the beholder'; 'works which are seen from a great distance do not appear as they really are'. This conception was transmitted to the Byzantines five hundred years later by Proclus's *In Euclidem I*. 'Skenography is the practice which teaches the artist how to ensure that something in his work should not appear distorted by distance or by height.' It was equally applicable whether the scene or image was represented in two dimensions on the wall or ceiling or in a fictional box space let into the wall—since Byzantine fictional space opens outward and downward into the real space before and below it in which the onlooker stands. It explains the

6 CHRIST UPON THE PATEN
[*p. 26*]

7   THE PLEDGE OF INCORRUPTION
[p. 39]

modern description of Byzantine figures as 'elongated' or 'stunted', 'thickset' or 'ascetic'.

Many generalizations on Byzantine 'psychology of style' have been based on photographs, but photographs are seldom taken from the stance presumed by the Byzantine craftsman. The Angels above the sanctuary at Haghia Sophia seem distorted in a detail photograph[27] but undistorted when seen from below at an oblique angle. It seems presupposed that figures in an apse would be seen at a distance from the centre of the church, since the sanctuary and all that lay beyond chancel screen or iconostasis was inaccessible to the people. If of the same size the outer figures at the two edges would seem more slender than those lying at a more normal angle of vision, in consequence they are made more thickset like the two Apostles at the edges of the mosaic in the apse of Torcello.[28] The lower portion of a figure in a vault or cupola was artificially elongated[29] to compensate for the fact that the upper portion on the curved surface stood at right angles to the optical axis. When cycles in mosaic or wall-paintings are depicted in two layers and both layers are intended to be seen immediately from below the figures in the upper layer are normally higher and broader precisely since otherwise they would have been perceived as smaller and narrower.[30]

The principles of these optical corrections seem consistent enough, but many were to survive in the Neo-Byzantine art of the ikon quite divorced from their original context. Even in the original context their application at times seems excessive to us, and perhaps this may be because our eyes are now conditioned to make a number of perspective corrections automatically.

It can clearly be only an assumption that the Byzantine saw exactly as we see. It is possible that their colour sense, like their tactile sense, was more vivid and perhaps more subtle than our own. In the 6th century Paulus Silentiarius describes the marble sheathing within Haghia Sophia as 'spring green from Karystos and many-coloured Phrygian where red and silver shine like flowers. Porphyry is powdered with stars. Crocus glistens like gold. Milk is poured on black flesh. Blue cornflowers grow among drifts of fallen snow.' [31]

This Byzantine colour sense may explain the rôle of the treatises on *Catoptrica* in their study of optics, since these provided devices for the reflection and refraction of light which could render changing colour tonalities more explicit. Too little work has so far been done on the forms of lighting chosen by the architect for the work of the mosaicists, painters, or marble-cutters in his employment—the use of small open windows set along the cornice of the dome as in Haghia Sophia; of thin panels of translucent alabaster as in the 'Mausoleum of Galla Placidia' at Ravenna; or of small circular panes of coloured glass like those of which fragments have been found recently at San Vitale.

But it is not only in colour sense that the Byzantine visual process may have been slightly different from our own. It seems clear that the Byzantines assumed that the human eyeball was mobile, was spherical in shape and had a concave retina. They could never have been satisfied with any system of perspective which presupposed that the human eye was a flat object gazing immobile at a vertical plane. Their horizon lines often seem curved even if only slightly, while often in the West the horizon has been conceived as a straight line.

It is once again becoming fashionable to assert that Hellenistic painters were addicted to linear perspective and to the use of the vanishing-point; much has been built on an enigmatic statement of Vitruvius: '*omnium linearum ad circini centrum responsus*'. But there is nothing to show that this centre of a circle which is the meeting-point of lines is the Renaissance vanishing-point or indeed that it is within the picture. In Hellenist and

Byzantine optics the straight lines that are the visual rays have their meeting-place in the eye. It is from the eye that they go out to touch the circle round it. Euclid, in his *Optics*, had defined visible dimensions in relation to the angles of vision that include them.

There seems nothing in common between the Byzantine visual process and that of photography; the result of the visual process is an act of mind that renders it articulate. Since man is the bridge-being between the worlds of *noetos* and *aisthetos* the vision that he sees, like the work of art that he creates, belongs to both. The visual rays are only the means of vision. Transient and flickering like all material things, they touch the surfaces of matter; yet from the shifting data they provide, the mind can construct a single vision and hold it temporarily immobile. Human hands are only the means of creation. They too belong to the world of matter, of *aisthetos*, though like human eyes as long as they are alive they are matter shot through with mind; the implements they use—pigments, or mosaic tessellae, or polished marble—are purely material. Yet through the hands the mind can construct an image which will be held temporarily immobile. Vision and Image are both passing echoes of the eternal immutability of God. Both possess material beauty in so far as they express an inevitable harmony of comingled line and colour. Such harmonies can be moulded mathematically. In his commentary on the first book of the *Elements* of Euclid, Proclus defines one form of progress from visible beauty to invisible Beauty as 'a transition from harmonies that are perceptible to the senses to those harmonies that are imperceptible'.[32]

4

The Hidden Meaning

IN BYZANTINE ART SYMBOLISM WAS TO TAKE TWO forms. The first was the representation of a scriptural scene that contained a twofold hidden meaning for the initiate, like 'the Old Testament Trinity'—the three men beneath the oak at Mamre in the eighteenth chapter of Genesis—or Christ raising Lazarus from the tomb. It is not accurate to describe this form of representation as allegorical, for an allegory is technically an extended metaphor and the Byzantine artist held that he was representing a past fact—there had been three angels entertained at Mamre, Christ had summoned Lazarus from the tomb at Bethany—but it was a fact which contained at the same time a deeper and more universal and also a more immediately personal meaning. The scene at Mamre conveyed not only the Inner Life of Godhead but the possibility for each to share in it through the Eucharist on earth, the scene at Bethany conveyed not only Christ's triumph over death but His summons to each sinner to leave the darkness and the stench and come into His light; 'Lazarus, I say to thee arise.'

The second form of Byzantine symbolism was based not on the scene but on the object—the vine or the peacock or the river. It was most commonly derived from the pastoral conventions of secular Hellenistic art. Each object brought with it a cluster of associated images.

Linking these two forms together there was the greatest of Byzantine symbols; not a scene but an object, both factual and scriptural—the Cross.

Considered quantitatively Byzantine art was never predominantly symbolic, even though it is possible that some conventions which now seem purely decorative were also

symbols.[1] But considered qualitatively the masterpieces of Byzantine art are predominantly those that contained and conveyed hidden meanings. No scene from the Old Testament inspired such a sequence of achievements as the three men at Mamre—from the Old Testament Trinity at San Vitale to the Old Testament Trinity still commonly attributed to Andrei Rublev.[2] In the Christ cycle this is paralleled by the Anastasis convention with its variant, the Descent into Hell, and by the Raising of Lazarus—all three containing the central Christian *mysterion*, rebirth and the conquest of death and sin. So also with the symbols derived from a non-Christian past, the vine tendrils that were to become the True Vine on which the Christian is grafted through participating in Christ, and the peacock which signified human flesh grown incorrupt through such participation: masterpieces at San Vitale, in the Chora, at Torcello.

Much that was most vital in Byzantine art came into being through the effort to apprehend and to convey a hidden meaning. Two peacocks are drinking from the chalice on the chancel screen in the cathedral of Torcello. The carving is most likely Constantinopolitan and 11th century. The exact mathematics of the composition, the tactile value of the surface, the balanced rhythm of the figures could satisfy Byzantine sense perception, but it could also satisfy another form of *aisthesis*—not beauty experienced only by the senses but Beauty apprehended through senses by Mind. When contemplated it conveyed a cluster of connected truths; the Christian had put on incorruption by drinking from the spring of living water and by partaking in the Eucharist. By so doing he had received the pledge of immortality and by so doing he had pledged himself to drink of the Chalice that Christ drank of and to be baptized with that with which He was baptized.

This conception of a content within an art-form can best be clarified by analysing in detail its ultimate origins in 3rd-century Christian symbols and homilies. It seems indisputable that much early 'Christian' art was only decorative, but the persistent popularity of a number of conventions can best be explained if they conveyed a hidden meaning to the initiated.

The earliest Christian paintings in the East that can be dated with some exactness are those at Dura Europos on the Euphrates.[3] The excavators there found an early-3rd-century private house which had been transformed into the headquarters of a Christian community in about 232. It contained a small room used for initiation by Baptism into the Christian Mystery, and decorated with paintings placed there before 256; the work apparently of two journeymen, the first Hellenistic in his approach and acquainted with some of the technique of illusionism, the second perhaps a local apprentice.

Five women were shown moving processionally towards the left. The number five suggests that this is a scene from Scripture, the five wise virgins going to meet the Bridegroom. But for the initiate about to receive Baptism it could have another and directly personal meaning. Much of 3rd-century homiletic teaching is compressed by Methodios of Olympos in his *Banquet*.[4] 'The five wise virgins refer to the one who keeps undefiled the fidelity of the five pathways of virtue—sight, taste, smell, touch and hearing—because she has preserved intact for Christ the five perceptions of her senses, causing holiness to shine forth from every one of them. Our body is truly as it were a lamp with five lights. The soul carries it as a torch to meet Christ her bridegroom on the day of resurrection, thus manifesting her Faith which leaps up brightly through her every sense.'

On a smaller scale there is a painting of a serpent and a tree, a man and a woman. Clearly a representation from Genesis. But it is precisely because Adam and Eve convey the concept of Christ and of His Church that they find their place in the conventional decoration of a baptistery. A commonplace in 3rd-century exegesis is also restated by Methodios in *The Banquet*. 'The Apostle could apply directly to Christ all that was said of Adam. It is in excellent accord with this that the Church has been formed from His flesh and bone. For it was for her sake that the Logos left His heavenly father and came down to earth in order to cling to His Spouse and slept in the ecstasy of His passion . . . cleansing her with the laver for that blessed spiritual seed which sows and plants; and like a woman the Church conceives of this seed and forms it.'

In another painting a woman is sitting by a well; a literal representation of the Woman of Samaria, yet she is also the Church, the Woman *Ekklesia*, waiting Christ's command to draw up from her well the living waters of immortality to give to those about to be christened.

In the vaulting, stars were painted against a blue background. This was to survive as a Byzantine convention and find its most perfect aesthetic expression in the 'Mausoleum of Galla Placidia' at Ravenna. It is not possible to be certain of the interpretation either at Ravenna or at Dura, but it seems likely that this implied the Kingdom of Heaven, in which the souls of the victorious faithful would shine as stars since they had become the gems of the *Ekklesia*. In *The Banquet* Methodios wrote of the *Ekklesia* as the Woman of the Apocalypse: 'She gleams in pure, unsullied and abiding beauty, emulating the brilliance of the lights. She is clothed in pure light for her garment. Her head is adorned with shining stars instead of jewels. Light is for her what clothing is for us. She uses the stars as we do gold and brilliant gems.'

If the choice of subject in the Dura painting may often be explained by a single mystic meaning underlying a representation of a scriptural passage, a threefold hidden sense was perhaps more common.

Examples that can be dated with some exactness are in the family vault of the Julii Tarpeiani beneath St Peter's.[5] This was redecorated in mosaic by a Christian owner, most probably about 260 or 270. On the east wall a man leaps from a ship into the mouth of a sea-monster while two other men still stand beside the mast with their arms raised in prayer. This must be Jonah and the Whale and the scene is so frequently repeated in 3rd-century painting and carving that its appeal must have lain in the truths it represented. In the presence of his disciples Christ the New Jonah goes down into Death to conquer it and to rise on the third day. Because of this the Christian, a new Jonah, can go to death while his companions pray for him, knowing that at the resurrection of the body he will be cast up whole on a new shore.

The common existence of a triple meaning in the representation of a scene is explicable enough as the result of 3rd-century exegesis. A belief in the hidden meanings within the Septuagint had been evolved in the Hellenized Jewish Community at Alexandria. The Epistle of Barnabas shows that it had been acclimatized in the Christian community by the year 130, and inevitably it was applied there to the New Testament canon also. During the 3rd century as Judaism grew more rigorous and more literal this belief came to be regarded as a Christian prerogative; Methodios of Olympos notes that the Jews study the Scriptures like butterflies settling upon leaves. The Christians study them like bees sucking the honey from a flower.[6] It would be an error to consider Origenist exegesis as characteristic of the 3rd century. Though Origen could not have written either earlier or later, his genius exaggerated the tendencies of his age rather than represented them. But though few exegetes would have agreed that the whole of Scripture could be interpreted spiritually none would have doubted that there were scenes from both Testaments that conveyed a multiple meaning. The scene itself was the body, the *soma*, and this found expression in the literal sense of the words. But the soul enclosed within the body was conceived as twofold, Mind and Spirit, either Logos or Nous, and Psyche. The meanings therefore are threefold. The body is immediately apparent to the senses; the soul and mind are to be discerned through contemplation. This conception could be shared in by the illiterate to whom it would be brought home by spoken homilies. It could be applied to the pictorial representation of scenes in Scripture as much as to the descriptive text. The craftsman re-enacts the literal sense; carving or painting the scene he makes the *soma*. This body encloses a soul and mind perceived only by contemplating the physically apparent. This will be found to provide a key to much Byzantine iconography as late as the 17th century.

Granted the principles of Alexandrian exegesis, all this is natural enough. But by the end of the 3rd century similar principles in selection and in interpretation would seem to have been applied to some scenes derived from the conventions of non-Christian Hellenistic art. I would suggest that such scenes can usually be traced to ultimately sophisticated and purely secular Greek art-forms, but they passed into a Christian milieu through 3rd-century proletarian art. Here they acquired esoteric religious associations. Further, there is normally some slight adaptation which links them with a passage in the Scriptures held to be related to either Baptism or Eucharist. Yet, as throughout Byzantine art, the sacraments were represented as united rather than as distinct parts of a single central *mysterion*, the rebirth into a new life and into another world. And already before Constantine the same scene could convey in symbol both the Eucharist on earth as the feast of the new brotherhood, and the heavenly banquet in the Father's house, the two linked by the sharing of the bread of life.

The representation of the common meal appears and reappears in Imperial Hellenistic art.[7] In the more sophisticated renderings of the scene the members of the *symposion* share some clearly marked characteristics; they are huntsmen or shepherds or philosophers feasting together. A wealthy patron might perhaps choose it as being decorative, and in such cases it may have been conceived as being secular and diverting like the huntsmen and shepherds that feast together on 15th-century Florentine bridal *cassoni*. But it gained new meanings as it passed outside a sophisticated milieu. To the *bourgeois* patron who commissioned it for his sarcophagus it may have primarily conveyed the sense of the brotherhood of a common guild made manifest at a funeral banquet. It seems probable that in proletarian art the common meal represented a sacred meal and had a number of varying but directly religious associations; a clear example of this is the Mithraic banquet on the relief from Konjica.[8] By the second quarter of the 3rd century it was being utilized in Christian proletarian painting and the conventions for the Byzantine Old Testament Trinity were to be derived from it.

The evidence once deduced from catacomb paintings as to the nature of pre-Nicene Christian art must be treated with caution; so much of the decoration of the cemeteries seems to have been placed there between the late 4th and the early 7th century when the cult of the martyrs had been fully established. Yet among many uncertainties Dr Fritz Wirth[9] has provided a clue through his analysis of the early-3rd-century asymmetric style of painting with its red and green linear décor. Following this it is possible to place a number of catacomb paintings be-tween 220 and 260. Among them is a representation of the common meal in the cemetery of Calixtus. Seven men are seated in a *symposion*, the figures sway asymmetrically behind a sigma-shaped table. Two fishes and some loaves are placed on it before them. Seven baskets are ranged in the foreground. The *symposion* scene has been adapted according to a conflation of two narratives in the Gospel of St Mark; the two fishes from Mark 6.38 and the seven baskets from Mark 8.8.

The Hertofile[10] sarcophagus from the Via Tiburtina now in the Museo delle Terme has been dated by Dr F. Gerke between 250 and 265. Two reliefs flank the medallion portraits. To the right Christ preaches from a boat upon the Sea of Galilee. To the left a group of men sit behind a sigma-shaped table, the one in the centre is drinking from a great cup, five loaves lie on the ground before them. That the loaves should be five again sug-gests the foreshadowing of the Eucharist at the feeding of the multitude. An illiterate scrawl above one of the six *symposion* scenes in the cemetery of Peter and Marcellinus also seems to infer some association between *symposion* and Eucharist: '*Agape da Calda Irene misce mi*'—'Charity give strong wine, Peace pour it out for me.' Yet surely none of these examples symbolized the Eucharist alone. As funerary memorials they would have suggested the Heavenly Banquet also and a sacred meaning could be found in the representation of the Fish.

By origin the repeated representation of the fish was no more specifically Christian than that of the *symposion*.[11] It was a commonplace in Hellenistic art as a decorative motif, as at Delos and at Lindos and so often at Antioch. Yet especially in popular art it had come to possess religious associations—like the fish god in Lower Egypt, or the sacred fish of Atargates or Anaitis—and there is sufficient literary and epigraphic evidence[12] to prove that when used by Christians it contained a hidden meaning. Again the meaning was twofold, the fish was Christ, the Greek for 'fish' (ἰχθυς) forming the initials of 'Jesus Christ, God's son, Saviour'; yet it also symbolized the baptized Christian called to be another Christ, swimming in the baptismal waters of the New Life, dying when removed from them. It might give any scene in which it was placed a sacramental meaning and that perhaps is why it is so often associated not only with water but with bread and wine. In what is probably the earliest of the *symposia* scenes in the cemetery of Peter and Marcellinus, three men are seated behind a table while a great fish is laid upon a tripod above a two-handled wine amphora. In the 3rd-century cycle of the Calixtus paintings a fish swims through the waters bearing on its back a basket of five loaves. In a common fisherman convention two fish swim together down the river. On seal-rings two fish are shown above a basket.

Perhaps the inner meaning was always doubled.. This Fish that is Christ is partaken of by the brotherhood on earth at their common meal, and the souls of the Christian dead partake of the Great Fish as they drink new wine at the table of their Father. Christ plunges down into the waters of this life and so makes them baptismal, bearing with him the bread of Eucharist. The Christian, the fish that is the Christian soul, can swim in the waters of Baptism for he bears with him the Bread of Life. The fishes swim together for they are linked through Baptism in Tertullian's phrase as *Pisciculus* to *Piscis*. Yet again, perhaps the fishes and the bread joined together might convey the link between Baptism and Eucharist as well as all that was fore-shadowed at the Feeding of the Multitude.

On occasion a slight adaptation makes a threefold meaning clear. In a convention derived from the vineyard scenes, two men carry a pole between them with grapes hanging heavily from it; there are other grapes by their feet.[13] The literal sense is surely the return of the two spies from Canaan bearing the Grapes of Eshcol. The first hidden meaning is that Christians, the servants of the New Joshua, bring back to the brethren in the Eucharist the first fruits of the Promised Land. But there is a third meaning; there are other grapes by their feet. The Lord, whom Joshua foreshadowed, has trampled in the winepress alone and because of that bears upon his shoulders the grapes that are a foretaste of the wine in the Kingdom of His Father.

In later Byzantine iconography scriptural scenes interpreted according to such exegesis were to mingle with symbolic renderings of secular art and with later echoes from classical mythology.[14]

5

The Phase of Integration

CONSTANTINE HAD INAUGURATED A NEW IMPERIAL headquarters at Byzantium on the Golden Horn. He was never to be forgotten as its founder. But not until a hundred and fifty years after his death did Byzantium come to possess the unique prestige that it was to retain throughout the Middle Ages.

Byzantium in the 4th and early 5th centuries was primarily the successor of Diocletian's Nicomedia as the centre of Imperial administration in the East. It could be paralleled in the West by Trier, by Milan and finally by Ravenna. But the whole Empire stayed united even when associate emperors shared in a single Imperial sovereignty. It was Rome not Constantinople that was still The City.

Western historians looking across the 5th- and 6th-century anarchy have tended to conceive 4th-century Graeco-Roman civilization as disintegrating. It is equally natural for a Byzantinist looking back on an unbroken continuity to see the 4th and 5th centuries primarily as a period of integration; in administration and in religion, in culture and in art-forms. For an art historian the development of the Byzantine civil service is a crucial factor and this was in itself the effect of political change.

At first it seems inexplicable that the Roman Empire should have survived in the Eastern provinces while the West sank into anarchy between 406 and 455, for the causes that led to catastrophe seem to have been equally common throughout the Empire as a whole. There was a diseased economy with its symptoms of excessive taxation, excessive regulation of trade and industry, and an oppressed and dwindling middle class. There was the rising pressure of German peoples against the frontier lines. There was the presence of German mercenaries in the Imperial armies, only slightly assimilated by Rome but increasingly holding the highest military commands. It was these *foederati*, like Alaric and his mutinous troops, who were so often to paralyse Roman resistance and to provide the barbarian invaders with efficient military leadership.

German *foederati* were as prominent in the army of the East as of the West. In 5th-century Constantinople Aspar combined the rôles of Stilicho and Alaric, while the younger Theodoric the Ostrogoth was to be more capable and ruthless than either. German pressure was as strong against the line of the Lower Danube as against that of the Rhine. It was the line of the Lower Danube that snapped first. There was an added danger to the East from the highly organized military power of Sassanian Persia. But the Empire possessed in Asia Minor a permanent reserve from which a native army could be recruited. The same system of taxation and restriction was enforced in the East and in the West, but the East retained a more vital city life as a legacy from its Hellenistic past. By the time of the accession of the Emperor Anastasius in 491 it was apparent that the Roman Empire would survive in the East, although no one who knew all the facts could have guessed that it would do so for nearly another thousand years.

The Empire that had been ruled by Constantine had survived; but it had survived altered. The extent of this alteration had been masked since the innovators among the 4th-century emperors, Constantine, Julian and Theodosius, had all been by intention reactionaries.

There was much that was classical about Constantine. One of his panegyrists had compared him to Apollo since he was 'young and joyous, health-giving and most beautiful'.[1] Perhaps that was how he continued to conceive himself until he died in his late fifties. To judge by the sculptures that he pilfered, his own tastes were for strictly classical art. On the most likely interpretation he came to power as the representative of a pro-*bourgeois* and liberal party in reaction against the innovations of Diocletian's Tetrarchy. He could do little for the *bourgeoisie* except to reassert its status;[2] the need for revenue was too great. But his new legislation was aimed to strengthen the traditional props of the classic Roman order, the family unit[3] and family power and property rights,[4] and was frequently coloured by liberal sentiments that seem derived from 1st- and 2nd-century Stoicism.[5] He was clearly a convinced adherent of the *Summus Deus*. He became at first an ally and then the lavish patron of the Christian Church, which he conceived as the association of the *cultores summi Dei*. It was only on his death-bed in 337 that he became a member of it.

His nephew Julian expressed and led a reaction in 361. In theory it was his aim to revive the cults of the Graeco-Roman gods and to return to the Principate of Marcus Aurelius. In fact there are many ways in which he was the first Byzantine emperor. Constantine and Theodosius were both Westerners, Julian was an East Roman, bred in Cappadocia, at Athens, and in Phrygia. It was Julian who first gave expression to Byzantine conservatism: 'Innovation I abominate above all things.'[6] Oddly enough, he was responsible for the first definition of the Byzantine conception of the religious ikon as neither wood nor stone nor yet the god himself.[7] His list of virtues includes those that had been inherited from the classic past like Temperance and Justice, but he adds two that were to become characteristically Byzantine—the quality that prompts a man when he should submit or withstand or co-operate with circumstance,[8] and the determination to do nothing at random.[9] Writing in a society that had recently become ridden by hereditary castes he fore-shadows the Byzantine administration which was to remain, in

8   THE IMPERIAL LITURGY
[pp. 56, 57]

9 THE IMPERIAL PRESENCE
[*p. 56*]

theory, a career open to talent during a thousand years. 'But when Plato says a man should "depend on himself" most assuredly he does not refer to his physique, his resources, his birth or his ancestry. These things indeed belong to him. They are not the man himself. His real self is his mind and his intelligence, that is to say the god within.'[10] It was Julian who developed the doctrine of *philanthropia* which prevented Byzantine sovereignty from ever being conceived as arbitrary even when it was conceived as absolute. A true prince will recognize that 'every beggar in the streets becomes an insult to the gods'.[11] He will be distinguished from 'the vulgar tyrant' as a 'guardian of the laws' and as 'a political architect'.[12] His actions will be governed by his love for his fellow-men.

Julian never suffered the *Damnatio memoriae* which was the fate of so many unsuccessful emperors. He was respected by his opponents; Prudentius, the Christian court poet of the Theodosian house, wrote of him, '*Ductor fortissimus armis perfidus ille Deo quamvis non perfidus orbi.*' He was revered by his adherents; Eunapios wrote of him that 'his had been a mind equal to the deity'. It seems likely that he had a lasting influence in those openly or secretly pagan schools of philosophy and good letters which provided the Byzantine civil servants with their intellectual formation until the reign of Justinian. Some at least of his projected legislation was enforced by Valentinian and Theodosius.

I have always found it harder to understand Theodosius, but possibly there is less to be understood. Perhaps he was only a very talented general from Spain, carried by tides he half perceived. He entered Byzantium as emperor in 379 and died in 395. It is clear that the faction that at first supported him was the same that had supported his father Theodosius, the *Magister Militum*—Roman army officers who detested the prevalence of

German barbarians in high command. What has been termed the 'philo-barbarism' of his later years was not noted by his contemporaries. It was perhaps more accurately the search for a compromise solution by which German military commanders would be bound to the administration as *foederati* in a characteristically Roman web of contractual obligation. His effigies show how much he continued to prize the Roman virtue of *gravitas*. He reasserted the principles of equity and trusted in a military discipline. His sumptuary legislation shows that he was intent on preserving the decorum of Roman dress and abhorred the use of trousers. He was no more intentionally a revolutionary than Constantine or Julian, though like them both he was intentionally a renovator. But he was responsible for the final establishment of the Christian Church as the State religion of the Empire[13] and for the final development of the Roman Principate into a Sacred Monarchy.[14] And his rescripts struck at the basis of the Roman order by weakening the family unit and the *patria potestas*.[15]

Yet the factor that most clearly differentiated the Eastern provinces under Justinian from the Eastern provinces under Constantine was not due to the individual decision of an emperor. It was the slow emergence of the Byzantine civil service.

The development of an elaborate bureaucracy in the Late Roman Empire was administratively inevitable. As Christian Lucas has noted 'the growth of the interference of the imperial bureaucracy in local concerns proceeded alongside the decline of spontaneous municipal government'.[16] Again unwise currency manipulations in the 3rd century had led to inflation and to spirals of rising prices which could only be kept in check by an elaborate and steadily increasing system of State controls. Finally, 4th-century legislation tended to regulate to the smallest detail the activities of every citizen.

The link between this expanding bureaucracy and the standardized study of classical good letters came to possess a lasting significance for Byzantine culture. An education in the classics had an essential rôle in the preparation for the Imperial service since it was conceived as a training both in correct expression and in correct conduct, '*et recte faciendi et bene dicendi magistra*'.[17] Julian had stated that 'those who train the young in ancient literature . . . should be of sound moral character and should introduce no opinions which are novel and at variance with accepted belief'. For a proper education brings with it 'a healthy attitude of mind and sound opinions concerning good and evil, propriety and impropriety'.[18]

This passage marks the development of a Byzantine 'Confucianism'. It was to be as closely related to a successful career in the Imperial service at Constantinople as Chinese Confucianism to the career of mandarins. In 357 the Emperor Constantius decreed that promotions in the administration were to be made according to the degree of knowledge of good letters possessed by the candidates for office.[19]

The history of Byzantine art is unintelligible if the tastes of this service are ignored.

It is a truism that Imperial patronage held the same function in the development of Byzantine art as ecclesiastical patronage in that of the medieval West or the private patron from the Renaissance to the late 19th century. Haghia Sophia was rebuilt by the Emperor not by the Patriarch. The very elaborate building programme at Ravenna immediately after the reconquest by the Byzantines was far beyond the resources of the local bishop. It seems clearly the act of the Imperial administration. It was only a Victorian phantasy that the ivory throne of Maximian there was commissioned by Bishop Maximian from an *atelier* at Alexandria. It is obviously Constantinopolitan, a gift from the administration intended to be at the same time a sign of Imperial benevolence and a visible token of the Imperial presence, like the beauty of the apse mosaic in the abbey church at St Katherine's on Mount Sinai or the intricate magnificence of the floor mosaic in the cathedral of Sabratha. As far as concerns work of the first quality, there is little evidence for the existence of the private patron until about 1328 when the Grand Logothete Theodore Metochites decorated the church of the Chora at Constantinople. In the 15th century John Frangopoulos was at least partly responsible for the paintings in the Pantanassa at Mistra. It should be noted that Frangopoulos like Metochites was a leading civil servant. Granted the elaborate structure of the Byzantine State it would seem naïve to assume that art-forms were much affected by the individual tastes of passing emperors. Imperial patronage means the patronage of the Imperial administration.

The continuity of the East Roman civil service from the late 4th to the middle 15th century helps to explain the continuity in Byzantine art-forms as well as in Byzantine culture. Both in outlook and in training there was much in common between the 14th-century Chief Secretary Theodore Metochites and the 6th-century Chief Secretary John Lydus, even though Metochites was far the cleverer man. The dominance of the civil service was only seriously challenged in the 11th and 12th centuries when a group of noble stocks seized the high military commands. In spite of the presence of well-trained professional armies, Byzantine civilization remained normally an essentially civilian society. Even the 10th-century Byzantine general with the sweet-scented pastilles for his tent and his travelling library on the art of war was a rather civilian character by comparison with the standards of the contemporary West.

Not only the ideals in education and administration but the

methods of recruitment may have helped to preserve the continuity of the Byzantine bureaucracy. The civil service was never
to become a noble class. To the end it remained a career open to
educated talent irrespective of ancestry. But the ties of local
association, cousinship and intermarriage must have been strong
and helpful. An autobiographical passage in the *De Magistratibus*[20] of John Lydus illustrates the method of recruitment in the
reign of the Emperor Anastasius and suggests an interesting
parallel to the emergence of academic dynasties in modern
Oxford and Cambridge. 'When I was in my twenty-first year, in
the consulship of Secundianus, I came from my native Philadelphia, which lies under Mount Tmolos in Lydia, to this blessed
city; and after much consideration I decided to join the
Memoriales of the Court and to don the girdle with them. To
avoid wasting the intervening time I resolved to attend the
classes of the philosopher Agapius, of whom Christodorus the
poet speaks thus in his volume about the pupils of the great
Proclus, "Agapius, last but foremost of them all." Under him it
was my fortune to study the first part of the Aristotelian doctrine
and to attend some lectures on the Platonic philosophy. . . . But
fortune advanced Zoticus, a fellow-citizen of mine who took
extreme delight in me, to the office of the Praetorian Prefecture
under the mildest of all monarchs, the Emperor Anastasius. . . .
Zoticus enrolled me among the clerks of his office, in which it
so happened that the most equitable Ammianus who was
nephew of my father occupied a distinguished position. . . . And
at the suggestion of the altogether excellent and reasonable
Ammianus, who all his life was devoted to learning and to
philosophy, Zoticus secured for me a wife who brought me one
hundred pounds of gold as her dowry and moreover excelled all
women who at any time have won a reputation for sobriety.'[21]

By the end of the 4th century three elements had fused

together and had created the East Roman bureaucracy—the fact of an expanding carefully graded and centralized administration, the conception of a knowledge of good letters as an essential part of its equipment, and the theory that as the service of the Sacred Monarchy it was itself sacrosanct. Promotion in it had become above criticism. An Edict of Theodosius I in 385 decrees that 'it is not fitting to discuss the princely judgement, for it is equal to sacrilege to doubt if that man is worthy whom the Prince has chosen'.[22] Status had become hieratic: 'If anyone therefore thrusts himself into a position to which he is not entitled, let him not defend himself by the plea of ignorance; but let him be tried for sacrilege as one who has neglected the divine precepts of the Emperor.'[23]

Of these three elements, the first was an administrative necessity, the second a Hellenistic echo, the third almost certainly the result of contemporary influences from the Sassanian monarchy in Persia. Similarly what has been termed the Oriental element in Byzantine art seems to be primarily derived from that Sassanid element in late-4th-century official art-forms which is so notable in the silver disk struck by Theodosius to celebrate his Decennalia in 388; in the diptych of Probianus; and in the sculptured representation of Theodosius at the base of his column in the Hippodrome. Like the changes in court ceremonial it is only a facet of the Sassanian influence in the conception of the Sacred Monarchy.

The Hellenistic conception of a divinity immanent in the ruler was no longer tenable in a civilization which since the 3rd century had come to accept the existence of a single transcendent God. The Emperor was now conceived as God's finite image and his sovereignty as the shadow of omnipotence. *Maiestas* had survived in a new context. Between 383 and 425 what had once been the Julio-Claudian Principate became a Sacred Monarchy;

State banquets in the Sacred Palace became 'divine feasts',[24] Imperial constitutions had already become 'Celestial Statutes'. The privilege of adoring the 'Sacred Purple', of 'touching Our Purple', of 'adoring Our Serenity' became increasingly restricted to a few.[25]

It was a great simplification to attribute all of this to Persian influences at the court of Diocletian. Dr Alföldi has shown that much of it was foreshadowed in the court ceremonial and court dress of the empresses of the Severan house.[26] Yet some of it at least was the result of the close contact between the administration of Theodosius and Arcadius at Constantinople and that of the Sassanian kings at Ctesiphon, where a developed autocracy and a complex hierarchy of officials was combined with a State religion that proclaimed transcendent monotheism.

The conception of the Adoration of the Sacred Purple by the few led naturally to that of the Adoration of the Sacred Image by the many. As the Principate becomes a Sacred Monarchy, official art becomes a sacred art and the Imperial portrait a cult object. As the Christian Church becomes the religion of the State, Imperial secular art provides the models of its art-forms. The enthroned emperor was the prototype of the enthroned Christ just as an enthroned empress was the prototype of the enthroned Mother of God.

The giant heads of Constantius and Valentinian, intense, immutable and remote, are clearly cult objects, the predecessors of the Late Byzantine ikon. By 388 the Madrid disk of Theodosius shows Sassanian elements integrated in a classic theme. Though in silver, it has many of the qualities of Persian rock sculpture both in its composition and in lack of depth. Theodosius I is enthroned with Valentinian II and Arcadius, the junior colleagues in his sovereignty, junior and so portrayed on a smaller scale.

A more complete synthesis can be found at the end of the phase of integration in the effigy, probably of the Emperor Justinian, on the Barberini ivory now in the Louvre.[27] Justinian is portrayed like a Sassanian king of kings, holding his spear and mounted on a rearing stallion while a supernatural power crowns him with victory. There is a calculated and hieratic disproportion in the figure scale, the men and women who crouch beneath him in their Eastern dress are rather bigger than his spearhead. Yet there is a Byzantine delight in optical contrivance; it can be calculated that the panel was intended to be seen obliquely from the right at an angle of forty-five degrees. There is a Byzantine delight in exact symmetry and *eurhythmos*— note the balanced sway of the wing feathers and drapery of the two genii who are also angels. The figures are moulded plastically in light and shade as in an older Greek fashion. The composition derives from the Hellenistic Baroque of one group of Severan sarcophagi.

It seems clear therefore that there was a Persian influence on the origins of East Roman official art as there was on the origins of Byzantine ceremonial dress. It was dominant among some forms of textile and possibly on cloisonné. I am now inclined to think, though I know well that it cannot be proved, that it may have had a crucial effect on the tonalities of Byzantine colour schemes. Perhaps Professor Strygowski (who was so often wrong) was right when he glimpsed a Mazdaean source behind the deep blue backgrounds of the 'Mausoleum of Galla Placidia'. But in figure-work, in composition and in iconography the Persian was never more than one element among many, and everywhere it fused with traditions that had long been current round the East Mediterranean. It seems to have been restricted primarily to the art-forms of the Sacred Monarchy.

The Christianization of the East Mediterranean world during

the 4th and early 5th centuries had been a gradual and probably a rather superficial process. But by the death of Theodosius II in 450 all temples had at least nominally been closed and the whole bureaucracy was at least nominally Christian.

The great sums spent by the Imperial treasury on Christian buildings were linked closely with Imperial legislation. Partly at least they were for propaganda. By them, as by the 3rd-century medallions, the policy of the Emperor was brought home visibly to his subjects. To judge from such fragments as survive, whole programmes were carried through hastily, expensively and rather nonchalantly. There is something fumbling about the official Christian art of this period. An admirable floor mosaic has been copied quite unsuitably on the 4th-century ring vaulting of Santa Costanza at Rome. The mosaic scenes in the Liberian Basilica that is now Santa Maria Maggiore are sophisticated and accomplished; they are probably early 5th century and the underlying design seems to have been commissioned from some manuscript illuminator trained in Hellenistic illusionist painting, but there can never have been any proportion between them and the building they decorated and it is impossible to calculate a stance from which they were intended to be seen.

Again, only one hypothesis can explain the composition of the mosaics in the cupola of the mid-5th-century baptistery of Neon at Ravenna; somewhere there must have been a 5th-century basilica decorated by two opposing lines of Apostles above the arcades of the nave, led by St Peter and St Paul and converging on a figure of Christ in the apse framed by curtains. The figures were divided by floral candelabra; the Apostles were derived from the Philospher convention on 3rd-century sarcophagi, the candelabra from Sassanian art. A copy of all this must have been commissioned for a form of architecture for which it was not designed. Again the mid-5th-century mosaic in the church of St

George at Salonika is of the first quality but its elaborate combinations in perspective would be more intelligible if it had been
planned for a flat surface rather than for a vault.

This apparent taste for the sumptuous haphazard has no
parallel in later East Roman Christian art, which is carefully
planned and measured. Possibly some of the Imperial officials
who commissioned these decorated buildings for the new State
cult were not very interested in the result as long as it was
sumptuous. This could also explain the tendency to over-
decoration. Scenes and emblems with traditional hidden meaning
are integrated into a new iconography which in terms of scriptural exegesis seems only to possess a literal sense and which is
modelled on the official conventions for narrative sequence and
for the representation of *maiestas*. There is a profusion of framework, scroll-work and foliage.

By 490 the process of fusion was still incomplete. Only one
surviving scheme of decoration fulfils completely all the demands
of later Byzantine aesthetic; that is in the 5th-century building at
Ravenna commonly called the 'Mausoleum of Galla Placidia'.

But in official art as in official culture the fusion had been
almost completed. There were of course other movements outside the influence of bureaucracy. There is evidence for the
survival of a proletarian Christian art, though this comes
primarily from the West. Between 350 and 490, Coptic and
Syriac cultures had developed independently of the Eastern
capital and were evolving a closely united system of art. These
factors were to influence later popular monastic art and the
conception of the ikon. This ultimate effect was probably
strengthened by the survival of pools of sub-antique art in
remote districts like Central Cappadocia. But the official and
religious art at Constantinople under Justinian stems from the
Graeco-Roman art of the 5th century. Many art elements that are

termed 'non-classical' could have developed stylistically in a classic milieu without any extrinsic influence. The marked weakening and at times virtual disappearance of the conception of plastic form can be explained as the result of a stylistic development long implicit in Imperial Hellenistic art and characterized by the excessive use of the drill in sculpture and by highlights in painting and by the zest to create colouristic surface effects. For the use of the highlights and of the drill may be defined as a 'technique to achieve illusionist semblances of the surface, while rejecting defined shapes and forms as carriers of firm bodies in real space'.[27]

'Non-classical' elements in Byzantine art may have been legitimate stylistic developments from the *Koine*, the common language of Graeco-Roman classical art-forms. Many sources have been suggested for them outside the boundaries of the Empire. Usually it is much more probable that they were due to stylistic developments within.

6

The Age of Justinian

THERE WAS NOTHING STERILE IN BYZANTINE CIVILI-
zation. Its first phase from 408 to 602 was one of the primary
creative periods in human history, in thought and in literature
as well as in architecture and art.

The creative thought of this period has often been ignored,
but no one who has studied them can doubt the speculative
strength and original vision of St Cyril of Alexandria and of his
opponent Theodoret, or the lasting and transforming influence
of Proclus and of Pseudo-Dionysius; the list could be lengthened
by quite forgotten names: Nemesios of Emesa, Leontius of
Byzantium, the Pseudo-Cyril, possibly John Philoponos. Roman
law, with all the crucial concepts explicit or latent in it, came to
the West through two Byzantine syntheses: the 5th-century
Theodosian Code and the Corpus Iuris of Justinian. Classical
literary forms like the epic and the dialogue still lived and the
reign of Justinian coincided with the final flowering of the
Greek epigram. Fresh literary forms were created in hymns, in
chronicles and in lives of saints. There was nothing sterile in a
literature which produced an orator as great as Chrysostom, an
historian as great as Procopius, poets as different and as great as
Agathias and Romanos.[1]

The parallel achievements in architecture were partly due to
the prestige accorded to the mathematician and the engineer and
to the fashionable zest for new mechanical contrivances. When
the great church of Haghia Sophia was consecrated at Constantinople in 537 it was admired as much for its technical daring
as for its mathematically perfect harmony. 'The like has never
been seen from Adam', it is 'marvellous and terrifying'. San
Vitale at Ravenna was consecrated in 548; Agnellus notes how

much it surpassed other churches not only as a building but as a work of mechanics.[2] For Haghia Sophia was only one of many architectural experiments: the creation of the five-domed cruciform church,[3] of the domed basilica,[4] of variants of the domed church with radiate plan,[5] of the final evolution of the basilica-type,[6] of new forms of citadels, aqueducts and cisterns.

Art objects at this period were judged by a double standard. They could be considered a part of architecture—as by Paulus Silentiarius in his description of Haghia Sophia—or objects in themselves, as in the epigrams by Agathias, Macedonius and Arabius. A mosaic was already considered as much a functional part of an architectural whole as differing coloured marbles and carved capitals. The verses of Paulus, like the treatises on optics, provide evidence for a new aesthetic of colour which took into account the play of light on changing tints. But when art objects are considered in themselves they are primarily praised for the possession of an intrinsic life. It is the 3rd-century standard of Plotinus: 'Why are living things the more beautiful?'[7] Arabius the Scholasticus praises a sculptor who mingles the *pneuma* with the shape.[8] Agathias writes of a figure that 'laughs in silence and would have spoken if he were not held in forgetfulness by delight'.[9] By both standards the costliness or rarity of the material used is also prized.

There is much literary evidence for the expenditure by the Treasury of great sums on decorated buildings. Precious art objects still survive in carved ivory and silk textile, gold and embossed silver; a trivial fragment of what once existed. The period of Byzantium's greatest wealth was from 408 to 602, and the Empire was never again to command the same revenues. From the 5th to the 7th century, Greece, much of the Balkans, Asia Minor, Syria, Palestine, Egypt and Cyrene and areas in the Crimea, the Caucasus and North Mesopotamia were ruled from

Constantinople. In the 6th century all Northern Africa was conquered, with Sicily, Southern Italy and South-east Spain, while
the Exarchate of Ravenna was established on the Italian shore of
the Adriatic. State ownership of all mines, of many factories and
of great domains as well as an elaborate system of direct and indirect taxation, made the Emperor at Constantinople the richest
sovereign in the world.[10]

Behind the elaborate building policy of the administration
there lay the conception of Imperial largesse. The Emperor's
power was in no sense arbitrary. He was conceived as the sacred
viceregent of God on earth. His sovereignty reflected God's
omnipotence. But the divine omnipotence was conceived as an
act of mind and love; all things were brought into being and
kept in being by His knowledge of them. Therefore the Imperial
sovereignty was an act of mind and love, exercised according to
the unchanging law of reason and finding its fulfilment in the
essential Imperial virtue of *philanthropia*, the love of man.
Imperial largesse was an expression of this *philanthropia*. Each
gift was an act of love and mind. And, in a fashion hard for
Westerners to understand, each gift was also an Imperial 'theo-
phany' by which the mind and love of the Emperor visibly
became manifest, even along the farthest boundaries of his
Empire.

In practice it is difficult to judge how far the objects of this
largesse were the Imperial choice or how far patronage lay with
the great officials—precisely because it is now impossible to be
sure how much power in practice rested with the Emperor and
how much with the Ministers of State. The Master of the Offices
was in charge of the Imperial Chancellery and had the functions
of a Secretary of State for Foreign Affairs, but he also had command of the bodyguard and as head of the *agentes in rebus* was
Chief of the Secret Police. The Praetorian Prefect was Chief

Finance Minister and President of the highest court of appeal; he had gradually gained control of the internal administration of the Empire. The Quaestor of the Sacred Palace was President of the Council of State and Minister of Justice; it was he who drew up the answers to petitions. The Count of the Sacred Largesse had direct control of the Treasury and of all factories and mines. The Prefect of the Sacred Chamber was dominant in the elaborate court and in charge of the finances for its upkeep. Each of the great ministers delegated part of his powers to subordinate officials who in turn were assisted by chief secretaries and *adjutores*.

In theory the Imperial sovereignty was considered as elective, the Emperor being conceived as chosen by the Senate, the Army and the People. In practice it had become adoptive, with a tendency for the succession to lie within the same family grouping, but though this was increasingly supported by popular sentiment there was never to be a doctrine of hereditary right. The achievements of Imperial power from the 5th to the 7th century had been due as much to able ministers such as the Prefects Cyrus of Panopolis and Marinus, the Quaestor Proclus and the ruthless financier John of Cappadocia, as to able emperors like Anastasius, Justin, Justinian and Maurice.

In the same fashion the age of Justinian was also the age of Theodora, of Belisarius and of Anthemius of Tralles the architect. Anastasius the Silentiarius was already sixty-one and a rising civil servant when he became emperor in 491. He was influenced by his wife the Augusta Ariadne and guided by his finance minister Marinus. Justin, who succeeded him in 518, was already elderly, and had been apparently a compromise candidate. He shared his rule with his quaestor Proclus and increasingly with his nephew Justinian, who succeeded him in 527 and reigned until 565.

Justinian was very consciously a Roman; though he was bilingual in Greek and Latin, Latin remained his first language. The old Roman ideal of *gravitas* seems to have influenced even the way he carried himself, with his thick squat body, his heavy powerful face, his steady eyes. Yet he was typically Byzantine in his serene belief that he was the viceregent upon earth of a God-head who was Transcendent Mind. His legislation suggests that with an always impersonal and sometimes ruthless benevolence he sought the welfare of his subjects even to minute detail. But this was a loveless burden and perhaps he felt divided from those he ruled by a gulf almost as wide as that between Creator and created. By custom, Imperial isolation could be tempered by the choice of an associate in the Sacred Majesty; Justinian's choice was Theodora. An actress, a professional beauty and an adept in the chess-play of Byzantine court intrigue, she married Justinian when he was already heir to the Empire and ruled in partnership with him as Augusta until her death in 548. She could be pitiless and at times coldly and elaborately cruel. She was as incapable of cowardice as of stupidity. So much of her quality seems conveyed by her reputed saying, during the attempted revolution of 532: 'Empire makes a noble winding-sheet.' Perhaps it is an illustration of the entrenched strength of the civil service that in spite of all this it was to take Theodora eleven years to remove the Praetorian Prefect John of Cappadocia from his office.

Military subordinates however could be chosen rapidly, used efficiently and dismissed with nonchalance. Belisarius was appointed to the great office of *Magister Militum* when only twenty-five. He defeated Persians and Vandals and Ostrogoths and Huns; he conquered provinces; he was twice disgraced; he died after three years of complete obscurity. In many ways he was an anachronism—the last of those 5th-century Roman leaders who had acquired from the German *foederati* in the

10 THE EMPEROR IN TRIUMPH
[p. 58]

11 Pastoral

[*p. 77*]

Imperial service some of the standards of the Heroic Age. Relying on his chosen band of heavily armed horsemen, delighting in his own prowess, deeply emotional and sporadically magnanimous, he seems an oddly Arthurian figure against the still-life of the court.[11]

The mathematician Anthemius seems more characteristic. He is perhaps the only Byzantine artist of whom we have personal knowledge. Anthemius[12] was born at Tralles in Lydia and belonged to that Greek professional middle class which had been for long the chief support of Hellenism in Asia Minor and which had recently provided many distinguished administrators and theologians. One of his brothers was a physician, one a surgeon, one a lawyer, one a professor of rhetoric; his father Stephanus was a physician. It does not seem that his work ever brought him much wealth—we know from Agathias that he lived in a flat at Constantinople[13]—but it brought him much prestige. Procopius describes Anthemius as 'the man most learned in what is called mechanical science, not only among the men of his own time but among all men for many generations back'.[14] Agathias writes that he 'had reached the summit of mathematical science'. In 532 Justinian chose him to design the new Haghia Sophia.

Anthemius is never referred to as an architect in the Western sense. Procopius describes his craft not as *architektonike* but as *mechanike* or engineering. Agathias writes that his *techne* was 'the application of geometry to solid matter'. The whole of Haghia Sophia, decorations as much as structure, is an application of geometry to solid matter. But Agathias adds that he could also 'make copies and as it were models of things that are'; this is the conventional phrase for paintings and sculptures rather than buildings and suggests that he was ranked among the *zoographoi*, the painters of the living. He was also admired for his experiments

with the effects of compressed steam, and it was this that led
Justinian to remark that he combined the powers of Zeus and
of Poseidon. The anecdotes in Agathias suggest that he had a
quality of vindictive craftiness which was prized by his contemporaries. He belonged to the fashionable Odysseus type.[15]

It seems clear from his writings that his one intellectual
passion was geometry. In a very Byzantine fashion he was
conscious that he was the heir of a great tradition that it was his
privilege to transmit. He wrote of one of his predecessors 'it is
not to be thought that we shall overlook the demonstrations
given by him, but we shall attempt to set out those which we
ourselves adduce; not as though we were putting them in com-
petition with his proofs, for that would be to make a swallow the
peer of swans, but because we are ourselves able to provide
further hypotheses for those who are interested in mathematical
studies'.[16]

The applied mechanics that helped to make him famous
seem never to have had the same appeal to him as geometry and
optics. Although he wrote 'research into such matters as
mechanics belongs fittingly and thoroughly to him who would
be called the son of the muses',[17] and basing himself on Euclid's
Elements 12. 15 searched for the centre of gravity in a cylindrical
column, yet his accounts of his own methods read very drably:
'When any solid body is to be raised to a height, the lifting is
effected more easily with mechanical assistance when a beam is
pivoted about its centre of gravity. . . . Any weight can be trans-
ported without effort and easily to any chosen position when it is
raised from the centre of gravity. . . . When the weights are not
placed in equilibrium and we do not take hold of the object by
the centre it is difficult to lift them, because the inequality of the
weights prevents a balanced movement.'[18]

Compare all this with his short treatise that begins 'It is

required to cause a ray of the sun to fall in a given position without moving away at any hour or season. Let the given position be at Alpha and through Alpha let a meridian line Alpha-Beta be drawn parallel to the horizon as far as the slit or door through which the rays are required to penetrate to Alpha. Let Beta-Gamma be drawn through Beta normal to Alpha-Beta so that it is equinoctial. And let there be another straight line Beta-Delta for the summer solstice and similarly let Beta-Epsilon be the winter ray. . . .'[19] Even the least mathematically minded will notice that this treatise has a passion of compressed thought quite lacking in his accounts of his mechanical contrivances.

Anthemius of Tralles was only the most prominent member of a group. There was the geometrician Eutocius who dedicated to Anthemius his commentaries on the *Conics* of Apollonius of Perga. There was Isidore of Miletus who worked with Anthemius on Haghia Sophia and was recognized as his successor. Isidore too was a mathematician rather than an architect; he was the author of the fifteenth book of the *Elements* of 'Euclid' and was to be referred to by Byzantine geometricians as Isidore our 'Great Teacher'. There was the younger Isidore who rebuilt the dome of Haghia Sophia. There was Eulalius who was remembered as responsible for the church of the Holy Apostles built between 536 and 545. There is the enigmatic figure of Julianus Argentarius who possibly had the same relation to San Vitale as Anthemius to the Haghia Sophia and planned and decorated it with mosaic and plaster-work and marble by applying geometry to solid matter; if this was so perhaps he also planned the church of Sts Sergius and Bacchus, since the same mind seems to lie behind both.

This is a group which in the 6th-century Byzantine social structure can best be placed among the civil service which provided them with their admirers, their patrons and perhaps their friends. Fortunately we have enough literary evidence from which to gain a uniquely complete knowledge of the tastes, beliefs and aesthetic standards of the 6th-century Constantinopolitan bureaucracy. It seems to have possessed some of the close-knit texture of a good Late Victorian club. The account by John Lydus of his recruitment into the service under Anastasius has been quoted in the last chapter. It continues with his account[20] of his retirement from it, forty years later under Justinian, with the title of *Clarissimus* and with the rank of a Count of the Second Class. 'I then proceeded to the Palace escorted by my most sweet comrades, and having received the distinction that is customarily bestowed by the Emperor on those who have completed their service I went back to my books.'

There was a quite unwarranted opinion that the service was on the decline. John Lydus notes[21] 'The lost signs of ancient grandeur are many and beyond count.' Formerly it was the custom 'to employ only the very finest paper in official business while the clerks were as resplendent as the paper that they wrote on. But now both are gone and they exact a most mean and miserable fee and issue leaves of grass instead of leaves of paper, with cheap writing that smells of poverty. All this has perished and departed never to return.' Perhaps this nostalgia for the past affected the approach to the new official religion.

It has often been stated that Byzantine art is essentially religious and reflects an essentially religious society and it is worth considering this point in some detail. Perhaps it was only scandal that the Praetorian Prefect kept vigils in a Christian church in order that he might pray there by night to the Hellenic gods.[22] But Procopius, Chief Secretary of Belisarius, was able to publish in the official history of the Wars 'there came as envoys from Byzantium to the Chief Priest of Rome, Hypatius, priest of Ephesus, and Demetrius from Philippi in Macedonia, to discuss a question of dogma on which Christians are divided and engaged in controversy. The point of the controversy I shall not mention though I am thoroughly acquainted with it. For I hold it to be a sort of mad folly to research into the nature of God. Even human nature cannot I think be precisely understood by man, still less so can the things that appertain to the nature of God. So let me shun this peril and pass these questions by in silence, if only to avoid casting doubt on things revered. For I personally will say nothing whatever about God except that he is altogether good and holds all things in his power. But let each man speak about this according to the knowledge that he thinks that he has, both priest and layman.'[23] This is the 3rd- and 4th-century cult of the *Summus Deus*. As the *Secret History* suggests it was quite compatible with a belief in demons, but it was very remote from the decisions of the Council of Nicea and from the rigours of official orthodoxy. It is true that in the *Buildings* Procopius writes of Haghia Sophia that whenever anyone goes there to pray 'his heart is lifted up to God' and that he deems that God is 'somewhere near and loves the place that he himself has chosen to dwell in. And this happens not only when he visits it for the first time; every time he goes there everyone gains the same impression, as if each visit was his first.' But he does not state that the Christian God was the God to whom he prayed in the church of Holy Wisdom.[24]

The Edict of 410 had been an attempt to 'Christianize' the administration. Perhaps it had not been enforced strictly; so much Late Imperial legislation was primarily the announcement of an official programme. In the 6th century it seems most improbable that any man could have reached high office without some participation in the Christian rites and liturgy. But such conformity seems to have been compatible with a certain scepticism as to Christian ethics and doctrine.[25]

Rufinus the Domesticus was head of one of the departments of the civil service under Justinian. He wrote 'let us bathe, Prodice, and garland ourselves and lifting larger cups drain unmixed wine; little is our life of gladness, then old age will stop the rest and death is the end'.[26] Julianus had been Prefect of Egypt under Justin; he wrote as his own epitaph: 'I have sung this often, I will cry it even out of the grave: "Drink before you put on this cloak of dust." '[27] Macedonius of Thessalonika, Consul under Justinian wrote, 'I know not whose I am, or who I am or whence I came.'[28]

Such scepticism could be combined with the decorous attendance at the Christian liturgy as an official duty and with an acceptance of the ancient gods perhaps primarily as a literary convention; Macedonius the Consul wrote: 'It was first on our slopes that the golden-haired God pressed the harvest of wine out of the breast of the grape.' But there is no evidence that the Imperial administration was integrally religious, and under Justinian there is proof that much of the art that its members commissioned and most admired was purely secular—statues of successful charioteers like Porphyrios, and of boy runners like Thyrinos, wall-paintings of chariot races, memorial portraits of the dead and advertisements of courtesans, scenes in beaten silver and perhaps carved intaglios.

In the *Planudean Appendix* of the *Palatine Anthology* there are twenty-eight epigrams on the bronze statue of the charioteer Porphyrios, son of Calchas, which had been placed in the Hippodrome by Justinian.[29] Many of these deal with Porphyrios rather than with his statue. Leontios the Scholastic wrote, 'Victory fell in love with the eyes and the chariot of Porphyrios'[30] and compared him with Anchises and Endymion and praised his form as god-like. The statue is admired precisely because of its life: 'The sculptor exactly portrayed Porphyrios in bronze, fashioning him as if alive.'[31] 'The sculptor made the bronze like unto the Charioteer.'[32] But it seems assumed that the sculptor cannot equal the greatness of the classic past: 'Who art thou, beloved Youth, with the point of thy chin just showing the down?' 'Stranger, I am Porphyrios.' 'Who hast honoured thee?' 'The Emperor, on account of my driving.' 'Who testifies to it?' 'The Faction of the Blues.' 'Porphyrios, thou shouldst have had Lysippus.'[33]

Classical statuary was scattered through Constantinople not only in public buildings and in the streets but in the gardens of rich men's houses—a civil servant displayed his knowledge of Pindar by placing his statue above a stretch of water.[34] Much of it consisted of Attic or Hellenistic originals brought from Athens or Delphi or Pergamum; there were also probably many Hadrianic copies. It was the fashion to revere them rather indiscriminately since they were associated with good letters, though there is some evidence that groups were more appreciated than single statues, perhaps because they conveyed movement. Often their subjects were only guessed—there are strange passages in the second book of the *Palatine Anthology*[35] composed about 530 as a description of eighty-three bronze statues in the gymnasium of Zeusippus. Great names were attributed to them, Lysippus, Polycleitus, Pheidias, Myron, Scopas. There is of course no sign of any sense of history. There was the Present, there was the Classic Past. All the Past was conceived as contemporary with itself.

Classical statues could be easily transferred to the new capital but not wall-paintings; perhaps in consequence innovations in painting were not only admitted but admired. For the most part 6th-century poems on 6th-century statues deal only with their subjects; 6th-century poems on 6th-century paintings deal often with their technique.

Under Justinian a series of paintings in encaustic were placed along a frieze of a portico of the palace. They represented famous chariot races during his reign. Thomas, apparently a Curator of the Treasury, wrote of one of them, 'I marvel how some artist's hand has painted the horses as if alive.'[36] An anonymous epigrammatist noted, 'The artist persuades me that I see Constantinus the Charioteer of the Whites alive.'[37] A painting of Faustinus winning a victory for the Greens was much admired; 'Had it not been for the strong roof, Faustinus the ancient glory of the Greens would have mounted racing to heaven—so like to life are he and his team. Take the roof off and he will reach the sky.'[38]

Yet even when the skill of the artist is most praised he remains unnamed. Agathias describes a portrait of the Byzantine courtesan Callirhoe, apparently the mistress of his friend Thomas, the Treasury Curator, 'I am Callirhoe, the versatile, whom Thomas goaded by his love has set in this picture to show what great desire he has within his soul; for even as the wax melts his heart melts also.'[39] It is Thomas, not the craftsman in his employment, who is considered as making this painting in wax encaustic.

It was customary in 6th-century Constantinople for courtesans, lyre-players and dancing-girls to have their portraits painted, apparently as an advertisement. They were probably publicly displayed sometimes with poems attached to them like that on the ikon of Marina the Singer: 'Pitiable are those to whom she does not unbend. But he whom she favours is a second Anchises, a second Adonis';[40] or the line on an ikon of a dancing-girl by Leontios the Scholastic, 'Rhodoclea Delight of Men, Glory of the City.'[41]

The genre has a special interest since it marks one of the sporadic emergences of the private patron in Byzantine work of good quality; the portraits must have been commissioned either by the subjects or by their employers. But no specimen has yet been discovered, though it is likely that some still survive under many over-paintings transformed into religious ikons. It would seem from the literary evidence that they were on wooden panels and were most likely a head and shoulders. At times at least they had a gold background—this must be the meaning of the epigram on the image of the lyre-player Anthusa: 'The son of Cronos poured himself on her as once on Danaë, but he did not come to her body.'[42] Occasionally they were criticized; Paulus Silentiarius wrote to a lyre-player 'the portrait does not justly show thy beauty'.[43] Frequently they were admired; three poems have survived[44] on the ikon of the dancing-girl Helladia of Byzantium who 'had reached perfection in the rhythm of music'. All must have been intended to portray individuals.

There is not sufficient evidence to suggest whether this was also true of a class of privately commissioned portraits of which we have literary evidence in the 6th century. This consists of funerary portraits which not only commemorated the dead but perhaps were thought in some fashion to perpetuate their presence. Again no such Constantinopolitan work is known to exist, though a number are likely to survive under over-paintings. But it is easier to surmise what they were like from the examples of Late Roman and Early Byzantine Egypt. They were probably head and shoulders or half-length painted in encaustic on wooden panels and commissioned from workshops which were perhaps as impersonal as those of 15th-century English alabasterers. It is likely that they followed set conventions—the old man, the youth, the girl—and represented embodied attributes rather than personalities. That they were a fairly common fashion is suggested by literary evidence such as the 6th-century poem[45] on the dead boy Eustathios: 'Sweet is thy ikon. I see thee in the wax. All who look on thy ikon blame Fate for quenching so much beauty.' Or the lines[46] of Leontios the Scholastic on the image of a dead physician: 'This is Iamblichos, sweetest among men, who reached old age without knowing the converse of Aphrodite.'

It is possible to reconstruct something of the aesthetic standards of 6th-century civil servants from their poems on secular art. It should be stressed that they were writing in a literary genre that had been popular in the Hellenistic Age and used epithets derived from such poets as Antipater of Sidon. But they were not only derivative. There are two new notes in the approach to natural beauty. The first is a delight in contrasted multiplicity of scene. Cyrus the Consul wrote of the view from the house of his friend Maximinus, 'often a man, leaning out from it slightly, has greatly rejoiced his heart seeing in all directions different things, trees and houses and ships, the city, the sky and the earth'.[47] The second is the reiterated pleasure in light; Paulus Silentiarius notes that he is 'struck by rays of sunlight from every quarter' and 'enveloped by the saffron-mantled dawn'.[48] There is a zest for rare marbles and for precious metals; it is a convention to regret that an image should not be made of gold.

There is a developed theory for which I have found no Hellenistic parallel on the relation between *phusis* and *techne*. *Techne*, 'craft', is procreative, bringing life out of the material. Nilus the Scholastic wrote to the mosaic of a satyr, ' "Why dost thou pour forth thy laughter?" "I laugh because I marvel how, put together out of all sorts of stones, I suddenly became a satyr." '[49] It is the right combination of *techne* and *phusis* that produces the work of art; hence Julian the Prefect wrote on the set-subject of Myron's heifer '*Phusis* and *techne* strove together in this matter of the cow so that Myron gave to each a prize of equal value.'[50] For *phusis* in Byzantine Greek had come to mean something more precise than nature. In contrast to *ousia* it meant Nature as a source of operation, a nature considered precisely in relation to its appropriate function. The right combination of nature and craft may be due to the craftsman's choice of right material and his capacity to unveil its essential function. A description of the polished marble in the martyrion of Polyeuctus in Constantinople states[51] that '*Phusis* had made to flower in the depth of the rock marvellous metallic veins of colour like flowery meadows and had hidden their glory, keeping them until they were revealed.' This seems the Byzantine approach not only to marble-work and to metalwork but to the choice of the cubes of a mosaic. This may explain why Agathias writes that Phusis is the mother of Queen Techne. The nature of the object contains the beauty. Craft is the midwife only.

But *phusis* can be considered not only as the nature of the material object used, but as the nature of the subject to be portrayed. Craft also combines with a nature when it gives it visibly the life that is appropriate to its function—in a 6th-century phrase 'pouring madness into a maenad', or 'making Prometheus suffer'. This is why Nilus the Scholastic praises the mosaicist at Antioch who made the satyr laugh and this is why Leontios the Scholastic writes in praise of a carving, 'though it is stone it endures pain'.[52] In this sense the *phusis* of an Imperial image is the Emperor's nature conceived precisely in relation to its essential appropriate function; by revealing it the craftsman uncovers Majesty.

7

The Official Programme

IN THE AGE OF JUSTINIAN, UNOFFICIAL SECULAR ART and religious art seem still quite distinct. Such Byzantine secular decorative art as has survived the 6th and early 7th centuries fits admirably with the literary evidence,[1] and there is a clear continuity between the boy feeding the donkey in the mosaic uncovered on the floor of the Great Palace[2] and the Silenus dancing with the Bacchantes on a 7th-century silver dish now in the Hermitage Museum at Leningrad. In both cases *techne* has been applied triumphantly to *phusis*, the craftsman has not only the sense of the nature of his material, but the skill to express the intrinsic life appropriate to the nature of the boy, the donkey or the Bacchante. But the line of development seems to run parallel to that of religious and official art. All forms of evidence suggest that secular decorative art was consciously Hellenist, quite unorientalized and unsymbolic. Its standards are those of surface-aesthetic. There is no sign of an attempt to express the mystery of a hidden meaning.

The approach to religious and to official art seems oddly different from this. The first book of the *Palatine Anthology* contains a poem by Agathias (*c.*536–*c.*582) in praise of a painting of the Archangel Michael. 'Greatly daring was the wax that formed the image of the Invisible Prince of the Angels, incorporeal in the essence of his form. . . . The man looking at the ikon directs his mind to a higher contemplation. No longer has he a confused veneration. Imprinting the ikon within himself he fears Him as if He were present. Eyes stir up the depth of the spirit. Art conveys through colours the soul's prayers.'[3]

The same book contains an intentionally enigmatic epigram which is best explained if it dealt with a representation of the child Moses being found among the rushes. 'An Egyptian Woman. A Hidden Child. Water near by. These are the proto-types of the Word to those that possess *eusebeia*.'⁴ 'To those that possess *eusebeia*'—*eusebeia* means something more than piety, it implies the capacity to focus intently upon the Divine. Only those who possessed it would be initiated by it into the hidden meaning contained by the scene and see the Gentile *Ekklesia* in Pharaoh's daughter, Christ in the child, Baptism and the waters of the New Life in the river by Him.

Another epigram seems to convey the same sense of the hidden mystery of an Old Testament scene that foreshadowed a New Testament fulfilment, since it probably refers to a repre-sentation of the Old Testament Trinity, Abraham's guests beneath the oak at Mamre: 'Here God had only the Human Form; later He seized Human Nature.'⁵

Poems on New Testament scenes suggest a variant approach. For these are not types; they do not foreshadow the Incarnation. They are episodes in the Incarnation which contain an eternal relevance for every Christian since they possess an eternal validity in the mystery of Reconciliation. But like the Old Testament their inner meaning will only be made plain to those initiated by *eusebeia*. There is an epigram on the water-jars at Cana. 'If the spirit of God possesses thee thou understandest the Miracle.'⁶ And another on the scene by the well in Samaria. 'This is no type. A God who is also a Bridegroom saves a pagan nymph whom He sees beside the water.'⁷

Such interpretations explain the choice of the mosaic scenes placed in the sanctuary of San Vitale at Ravenna in about 549. Contemplated with *eusebeia* they contain multiple meanings. Abel offers his lamb, Abraham prepares his sacrifice, Melchisedek brings the bread and wine; above them God's hand signifies His Presence and His acceptance. These are not allegories, they are the representations of scenes which were held to have taken place; but they have a direct relevance to the Sacrifice that will take place beneath them at the altar. There is a clear reference to one of the oldest of liturgical prayers that God should accept the eucharistic offering 'as thou wert graciously pleased to accept the gifts of thy just servant Abel and the sacrifice of our patriarch Abraham and that which thy High Priest Melchisedek offered to thee a holy Sacrifice, a spotless Victim'. They contain moral teaching for every Christian since all are called to make their oblation. Both aspects are only there since the three sacrifices were held to be types foreshadowing the Sacrifice on Golgotha. Yet Melchisedek the King also foreshadows Justinian the new Melchisedek who leads the offertory procession in a lower mosaic. This is why Melchisedek wears the Imperial purple and the Imperial shoes and chlamys while Justinian carries in his hand the gold bowl with the sacrificial bread.

In San Vitale religious art and official art interpenetrate and both have inner meanings. Above the sacrifices of Abel and Melchisedek, Moses the shepherd tends the flock of Jethro and then bends before the burning bush. On the opposite side Moses comes down the Mountain bearing the Tables of the Law. Writing under Justinian, Cosmas Indicopleustes in the fifth book of his *Christian Topography* had analysed the story of Exodus as the type of man's redemption from the servitude of sin. But Moses is not only the type of the Good Shepherd, he is the type of Justinian the Law-Giver. The mosaics below, of Justinian and Theodora and the officials of their households, are among the supreme masterpieces of Byzantine official art but they are religious art as well. The Augustus and the Augusta bear the eucharistic oblations to the altar and through their images are perpetually present at each sacrifice.

In the 6th century, official art even when outside a church

seems to have shared in the conventions for religious art-forms. It normally possessed a symbolic meaning. The sixteenth book of the Greek anthology, the *Planudean Appendix*, contains a number of epigrams in praise of a bronze equestrian statue of Justinian that had been placed in the Hippodrome. The approach is of course quite different to that for the neighbouring bronze statues of successful charioteers. The Imperial Image is conceived as a perpetual re-enactment of the victories over Persians and Goths. 'Thy might, Justinian, is set on high. May the champions of Persia and the Scythians be prostrate for ever on the ground.'[8] 'The Bronze from Assyrian spoils moulded the horse, and the monarch, and Babylon perishing.'[9]

From the 4th century it had been held that the Emperor was in some fashion present through the official image that was his proxy; the site chosen for it had therefore an especial significance. Thus it is noted in the 6th century that the Emperor Justin's statue had been placed by the harbour to bring calm to the waters[10] and that the statue of his wife Sophia was placed by the law courts. A similar significance was attached to the exact siting of the images of living great officials who shared the burden of Majesty. Agathias wrote a poem when his friend Thomas the Curator had had his image commissioned by his subordinate Treasury officials and placed by those of Justinian and Theodora. 'Thomas, blameless Curator of the Ecumenical Emperor, is placed close to the Sacred Pair that in his ikon he should have a place close to Majesty.'[11]

Two poems by Leontios the Scholastic illustrate the tendency to look for hidden meanings in official portraiture. The first is in praise of an ikon of Gabriel the City Prefect with its elaborate parallel to the sun.[12] The second praises the ikon of Kallinikos the Cubicularius whose beauty had won its victory as he soothed the Emperor within the bedchamber. Some 6th-century official

art seems to have been as elaborately charged with inner meanings discernible to the initiate as any scriptural scene. In the
Planudean Appendix there is a poem in praise of the image of a
certain Peter.[13] It was apparently a fairly elaborate ivory in which
the central figure had been gilded. 'Behold Peter in his golden
robes. Provinces stand by him. There is a Witness to the East.
There is the Witness of the Purple Shell.' 'The Witness of the
Purple Shell' implies that Peter held the consulate; 'Provinces
stand by him' implies that he was a Prefect; 'The Witness to
the East' suggests that he was *Praefectus Orientis*.

Up to 540 the series of Consular Diptychs in ivory seem to
represent this type of official art.[14] They are cult images distributed in order that the Office should be honoured in its holder.
The emphasis is therefore on the official insignia, conceived as
outside space and time. The Official, often barely individualized
and frequently flanked by emblematic figures, gazes full face
upon those who would honour him. It is a hieratic art linked
with later Byzantine coinage but far closer to the nearly contemporary Sassanian rock carvings at Tak i Bostan than to any
Roman coins. It seems likely that such ivories were commissioned from an Imperial workshop in considerable numbers
and at the expense of the Treasury.

It is possible that there was a rather similar origin for the
Purple Codices. These are fragments of manuscripts *de luxe*:
the pages have been dyed purple, the script is either in gold
lettering as in the Sinope Codex at the Bibliothèque Nationale in
Paris, or in silver as in the Genesis at Vienna. Sometimes a
purple codex would not be illustrated, as in the Purple Gospel,
two folios from which were once bound with the Vienna
Genesis; more normally there were paintings on the lower half
or quarter of each page placed according to a technique evolved
from that of the illustrated papyrus roll.[15]

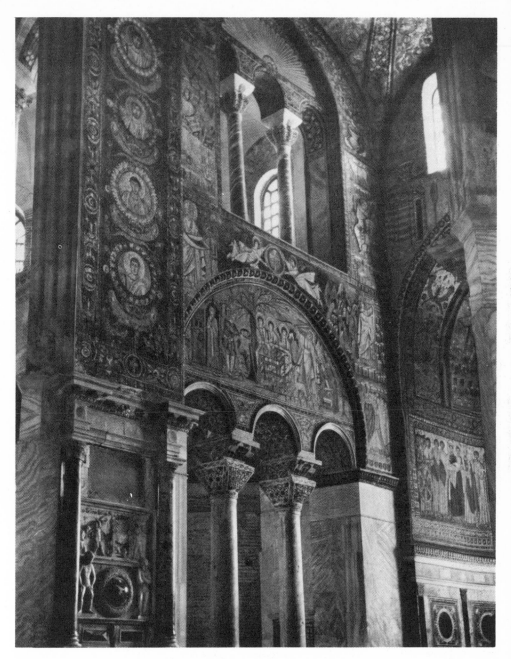

12   THE CHURCH OF ST VITALIS
[*pp. 79, 80*]

13   THE THRONE OF MAXIMIAN
[*pp. 53, 83*]

There has been much argument on the provenance of such manuscripts. Antioch? Alexandria? A centre in Syria? A centre in Anatolia? But I have long been inclined to hold that the clue common to them all is the use of the purple dye. For it was this which would mark each for the recipient as an Imperial gift. Even if there were private patrons wealthy enough to commission such gifts (and at least in decayed 6th-century Antioch this is excessively unlikely) it is not impossible they might have exposed themselves to a capital charge by such misuse of the Imperial colour. It is more likely that each purple codex, like the ivory throne of Maximian, was a gift commissioned from a workshop at Constantinople by the Imperial administration, perhaps to be sent to a cathedral that the Emperor had either built or restored. The unilluminated Purple Codices, like the Gospel book from Caesarea, may well have been used for public readings from the Scripture in connexion with the celebration of the liturgy.

Those that are illuminated must have had a different purpose. The paintings were not intended to illustrate the text; the text was intended to explain the pictures. Texts are often too freely rendered to have been intended to have been read aloud or studied; in the Vienna Genesis passages from the Septuagint are condensed or omitted. A clue to the use of these manuscripts is provided by modern Ethiopia, where some Byzantine customs still seem to be preserved like flies in amber. In 1951 in the abbey of the Sun at Cusquam above Gondar I found an illuminated manuscript *de luxe* of the Miracles of Mary chained to a lectern. The Empress Iteghe Mentuab had given it to Cusquam about two hundred years before. The format was oddly similar to the illustrated Purple Codices. One of the Elders of the monastery turned the pages slowly as he contemplated the painting.

Perhaps the pictures in the illuminated codices were intended to be used for meditative prayer as were some of the later ikon cycles. It would have been like the later Western use of the visual imagination on the sequence of mysteries in the rosary. The Codex at Rossano would provide the visual meditations on the pericopes from the Gospel read aloud during Lent. In the Sinope Codex the eyes would pass from the Old Testament type to its New Testament fulfilment.

But even if this is an essentially religious art, there is nothing to suggest that the artists were primarily religious. It is clear that they worked in groups; it has been calculated by stylistic analysis that either six, seven or eight painters collaborated on the Vienna Genesis. But it is only a phantasy that they may have been monks. It is far more likely that they were the staff of a large workshop which produced paintings on secular or religious subjects to order.

Fragments survive from three masterpieces of this genre. The Codex Purpureus at Rossano in Calabria, the Sinope Codex at Paris and the Genesis at Vienna may be considered as a group.[16] Though it is of course impossible to dogmatize as to the dating of the group, sometime between 527 and 565 seems not unlikely. It might be possible to reconstruct from internal evidence how such one manuscript came into existence. The Vienna Genesis can be taken as example.

Let us suppose that it was decided to send a Genesis picture book as an Imperial gift to some church in the provinces. It might be part of the Imperial policy of *kosmesis*, the adornment of churches which is so characteristic of the reign of Justinian. The expense might be borne ultimately by the Count of the Sacred Largesse, but such a trivial task would be entrusted to a subordinate official—perhaps one of the *palatini* employed in the central Finance Department. The gift would be needed by a fixed date, a 'Largesse Giving', possibly the following Easter. A purple codex would be prepared at an Imperial scriptorium. The Vienna Genesis was probably designed to contain 200 illustrations on 100 pages (of which 47 pages survive). Each sheet was 30.4 to 32.6 cm. high and 24.5 to 26.5 cm. broad and was definitively divided between a script and a picture area. The choice of the subject of each painting may well have been made at the scriptorium. When the sheets were prepared they were divided among two calligraphers who drew the uncials in silver; the first is the scribe of ff. 1–16, the second of ff. 17–24. The sheets were then sent to an *atelier* in Constantinople where they were distributed between five master-craftsmen, two of whom had apprentices working under them. They were then returned to the scriptorium for binding. How far were these painters copyists? One of them surely had genius—the Master who painted the blue floods swirling round dark Ararat and the men and beasts drowning in it. All were accomplished. There is sporadic evidence that they were painting hastily. Clearly they had pattern books and figure books, possibly in roll-form, but the pictures in them probably consisted of single figures or small scenes traditional in Hellenistic art; certainly there was a River God (who becomes Noah), a philosopher discoursing to his disciples beneath a tree (these are to be Noah's sons), a man sitting by a sun-dial, details for pastoral idylls. These were incorporated rapidly. But there is in fact no evidence that there was an earlier painted Genesis. Historically it seems more likely that the artists of Justinian created Christian archetypes rather than that they transmitted them.

All this is only a tentative reconstruction but at least it will explain every known fact. Stylistically it seems certain that the painters of the Purple Codices were not exclusively or even primarily illuminators; in the Vienna Genesis the work of the

First Master suggests a vault mosaic, that of the Fifth Master a wall-painting. The designs in their pattern books could also be used on floors or on walls for secular or for religious purposes.

The use and contents of a pattern book of this period can be illustrated from a discovery made in 1956 at Qasr el Lebia in Cyrenaica. In the 6th century this was the small episcopal see of Olbia and in 539 it was renamed in honour of the reigning Empress as the New City Theodorias. A mosaic floor was found in the nave of one of its two churches. It consists of fifty square panels each containing a different subject. It is only a work of the second order but the contrast between it and the roughly built church walls of stones set in mud suggest that it was an Imperial Benefaction given to celebrate the renaming. An inscription dates it to 539. It is most easily explained if it is a copy of a pattern book. The subjects could have been reproduced in any medium and combined in quite different compositions: some, like the classic river gods, have been deliberately Christianized and renamed after the four rivers of Paradise. Some, like the peacock, the two fish, Orpheus, the shepherd, perhaps the deer, had long contained a Christian hidden meaning. But the majority, like the satyr and the merman, animal combats and hunting scenes, the Pharos of Alexandria and the naked nymph Kastalia, can have had no religious or indeed symbolic sense.

Under Justinian there were three elements in the Imperial patronage of architecture and art: *ktisis, ananeosis* and *kosmesis*; 'foundation', 'renewal' and 'adornment'. At Qasr el Lebia they are personified as women. *Ktisis* holds the Imperial charter, the garland and the laurel spray. *Ananeosis* chooses fruit as she sits jewelled beneath the Imperial canopy. *Kosmesis* brings incense and roses. All three could have been depicted equally in a church, a law court or a public bath.

Procopius in his *Buildings* described the official policy of

Foundation and Renewal which was carried out by Justinian throughout the Empire, partly at the expense of the Treasury and partly surely through local forced labour. Much of the *kosmesis*, the Adornment that accompanied it, could be provided by Imperial workshops at the capital—portable ivories like the throne of Maximian at Ravenna and the Archangel Michael now in the British Museum, or beaten metalwork and textiles.

Paulus Silentiarius describes a hanging placed by Justinian in Haghia Sophia.[17] The most reasonable interpretation of his hexameters is that it consisted of a central image of Christ flanked by those of St Peter and St Paul and bordered by representations of Imperial Benefactions. Clearly it was a silk textile embroidered with gold and silver metal thread. It is noteworthy that it is primarily praised for its colour effects: 'The web, the produce of the worm from distant lands, changes its coloured threads of many shades; on it the form of Christ is wrought skilfully. Like the rays of rosy-fingered dawn, a tunic shimmering with gold flashes down to the Divine knees, a cloak deep red from the Tyrian shell covers the right shoulder . . . and the whole robe shines with gold, for a thin gold thread is led through the web. . . . On either side stand the two Messengers of God, and both the cunning web has clothed in silver. . . . On the extreme borders of the curtain shot with gold an art beyond speech has figured the works of *philanthropia* of the Kings of the City.'

Silk could only be imported from China until late in the reign. Even when it was woven within the Empire it would still be considered more precious than the conventional woollen decoration on a linen ground and was often used only as a small purple panel inserted in a Robe of Honour. Again it seems likely that the purple dye was already a monopoly of the Imperial workshop. Textiles could be sent as gifts either to churches or to individuals. Religious and secular motifs would seem to have

been used indiscriminately in their decoration. Representations
of the Annunciation and of the Nativity are repeated within
circular frames on a silk at the Vatican, the colours are green and
white and brown-gold upon a golden ground. On a fragment in
the Musée de Cluny a charioteer driving four horses is repeated
in a circular frame; the design in green-purple and the chariot
golden. Both are most probably Constantinopolitan and may be
of this period.[18] It seems likely that textiles were judged by the
same standards as mosaics, marble panelling, ivory-work and
carved capitals.

Literary sources suggest that the 6th-century ideal of
kosmesis consisted of the use of a precious material which conveyed multiple colours in a mathematical proportion. The four
colour groupings that were considered to bring most delight
were White, Green, Purple and Gold.[19] Purple and Gold were
to retain their appeal partly perhaps through association with
Imperial Majesty and with the Precious.[20] Blue was to be
favoured later. White and Green are especially characteristic of
the age of Justinian—like the white figures against an emerald
background in the upper mosaics in San Vitale.

White was considered as positive not negative, it included
silver[21] and two shades of ivory as well as marble and white
pigment. No object within Haghia Sophia would seem to have
given so much aesthetic delight as the great pulpit, the *ambo*;
Paulus Silentiarius states that by it 'the delight of beauty is
brought to the eyes', and that by it 'the heart is warmed with
joy'.[22] Though it was 'crowned with golden ivy-leaves powdered
with the dust of sapphires'[23] an especial beauty lay in the fact
that its ivory was inlaid with silver.[24] This would have brought
together three variants of white, since Paulus Silentiarius notes
two colours in its ivory. 'Sometimes the ivory has the choicest
tint of a pale crocus, sometimes the tint of the light creeping

round the pointed horns of a new-born moon.'[25] These variations in colour were arranged rhythmically.[26] Paulus Silentiarius states that 'intertwining circles wind under other circles' and draws what appears to be a parallel to 'the mazes of the Pyrrhic dance'.[27]

Green also was prized because of its variants, and these variations were most admired when they seemed to be reflections thrown up from some inner depth; for the highest praise of any green object was to compare it to an emerald.[28] Paulus Silentiarius writes in the first part of his *Description of Haghia Sophia* (lines 152 et seq.) of the various tints of green: 'who turns to the fresh green marble below seems to see the flower-bordered streams of Thessaly . . . a vine with green tendrils . . . the deep blue peace of summer seas; . . . above porphyry columns bright in their bloom stand others from Thessaly, splendid flowers of fresh green; . . . six columns, like the fresh green of an emerald, support untired the weight of wall, and these again are carried on strong columns; . . . glittering jewels of Thessalian marble with capitals above them like locks of golden hair'.

In the interior of 6th-century Haghia Sophia the dominant colours seem to have been white and green and gold. Attempts were made to break the monotony of the gold. Both in the description of Haghia Sophia and that of the martyrion of Polyeuctus gold is described as beautiful when it shimmers or when it glitters;[29] the effect could be achieved by placing the gilded mosaic tessellae at slightly varying angles, by occasionally interspersing them with semi-precious stones, carnelian or onyx and by a careful study of light reflections.[30] Procopius in his *Buildings* wrote that it was impossible to describe accurately the gold and gems in Haghia Sophia and that 'the reflections of the gold upon the marble are surpassing in their beauty'. Paulus Silentiarius states that looking upwards a man could see 'the shimmer of the tail feathers of a peacock with its countless eyes'.

To the anonymous author of the description of the martyrion of Polyeuctus the climax of its 'glittering elaborate beauty' was its golden dome.[31]

It is more difficult to determine the exact meaning of purple for the Byzantines. In the account of Haghia Sophia in the *Buildings* Procopius distinguishes it from 'glowing red': 'Who could tell of the beauty of the columns and marble with which the church is adorned? . . . who would not wonder at the purple tints of some and the green and the glowing red and shining white? . . . nature like a painter has used the strongest contrasts of colours.'[32] It may be suggested tentatively that the purple tints included any colour which had been mingled with the Imperial dye, 'the Produce of the Tyrian Shell'—purple-red, purple-brown, purple-green, purple-blue. Fragments of small circular panes of a purple-blue glass have recently been found at San Vitale; most probably they were used to reflect a purple tint on the vine tendrils in white plaster-work found at the same time.[33] But of all the purple tints, purple-red was the most common and presumably also the most prized since it was the colour of the Imperial vestments.

According to the conventions of 6th-century Byzantine *kosmesis* there were four ways in which the craftsmen could apply colours to adorn the interior of a building. Paulus Silentiarius has described three systems of decoration in Haghia Sophia in the second part of his poem. The first was derived from Hellenistic wall-painting: though some of its motifs like the Vine had acquired a Christian symbolism, most of them were probably purely decorative and secular;[34] 'on the flat surface of the walls intertwining curves are laden with fruit and baskets and flowers and birds sitting upon twigs',[35] and here was the curved pattern of a 'twining vine with shoots like golden ringlets'; 'such ornament as this surrounds the church'. The tendency is to describe this system geometrically and there was another system which was purely geometric: 'the tool has formed dazzling circles, beautifully wrought in skilled symmetry by the hand of the craftsman'.[36] But there were also isolated images of the Mother of God and of the Apostles: 'In other parts art has painted the Mother of the God Christ, Vessel of the Eternal Light'; 'Nor had the craftsman forgotten the forms of those others whose childhood was with the fishing basket and the net.'[37]

Only these isolated religious images followed the Greek classical tradition as defined by R. G. Collingwood in which the object is related to its space as a statue is related to its niche or a portrait to its frame.[38] It would seem from the contemporary descriptions that in 6th-century Haghia Sophia changing colours were coterminous with the space that they covered. Art and architecture were as fused there as in the 'Mausoleum of Galla Placidia' at Ravenna. Therefore the greater part of the *kosmesis*, the Imperial adornment, could only have been supplied by workmen on the site.[39] Mosaic-workers from the Capital may well have been loaned to San Vitale at Ravenna or to the monastery on Sinai as part of the policy of Imperial Benefactions.

Very little is known of the organization of the Imperial workshops at Constantinople. A Rescript of 374 preserved in the Code of Theodosius II[40] instituted a body of *picturae professores* with the function of decorating public buildings and executing the Imperial Image (*sacros vultus efficiendos*). Under pain of sacrilege, municipal authorities were obliged to recognize the privileges of its members: it possessed rent-free offices and it was exempted from providing official hospitality. But it included slaves as well as free men since it is stated that its free members must receive adequate payments. Such a body recruited from the abler free craftsmen and also by forced labour may have survived until the 10th century; thus in the early 8th century Theodore of Studios writes of Arcadius who, though a noble and a monk, was condemned to labour as a weaver on the Imperial looms.[41] It could have been the source for the mosaicists and painters who seem to have formed part of Imperial embassies until well into the medieval period. But all this is only a tentative hypothesis.

On any hypothesis it seems certain that architects, builders and adorners worked together as a unit during the building programme of Justinian. This programme of *ananeosis*, or renewal, was essentially a practical one as is repeatedly stressed in the *Buildings* of Procopius.

Perhaps it should be stressed again. Much has been written on the religious symbolism of the 6th-century dome; but the evidence can be reduced to worn literary metaphors in which it is compared to a helmet or the sky. It has become the custom to contrast the structural energies of growth in Gothic architecture with the Byzantine conception of a 'building developing downwards . . . in complete accord with the hierarchical way of thought'. It has been stated that for the Byzantine 'columns are conceived aesthetically not as supporting elements but as descending tentacles or hanging roots'.[42]

This is not a defensible antithesis. The 6th-century panegyric on the martyrion of Polyeuctus in Constantinople notes how 'it rises from its deep-rooted foundations, running up from the ground and aspiring to the stars of heaven'.[43] The decoration of a church could be described both upwards and downwards. And like Jacob's, the ladder of hierarchy could be ascended as well as descended.

Sixth-century Byzantine architecture was admired not for its symbolism but as applied geometry. In the fifth book of his *Historia* Agathias describes the improvement on the work of Anthemius of Tralles and of Isidore of Miletus that had been introduced by 'the young man Isidore'—'making these arches wider so as to be more in harmony with the others he made the equilateral symmetry more perfect'. He and his craftsmen 'were able to cover the measurelessness of empty space and to seal off some of its extent to form an oblong design', and working 'along the hemisphere . . . this also became of a better curve in every part agreeing with the line'. In Haghia Sophia 'it is the art that appears everywhere that makes men to contract their eyebrows'. Its beauty consists in the fact that it is so 'admirably a single harmonious whole'. Procopius writes of Haghia Sophia in the *Buildings* that 'a spherical-shaped Tholos standing upon a circle makes it exceedingly beautiful'. But it is 'through the harmony of all its measurements' that 'it is distinguished by indescribable beauty'.[44]

The conception of a religious symbolism in church architecture was to develop after the Iconoclast controversy of the 8th and early 9th centuries; it would come with a deeper sense of the religious meaning of an image. But the literary evidence shows that Byzantine art in the age of Justinian was not predominantly religious; it has only been thought so because of the accident that some of its church decoration survives but none of the decoration of its palaces, its law courts and its baths. Perhaps the best emblem for its art standards can be found on 6th-century capitals: the wind-blown acanthus.

8

The Evolution of the Image

THE EMPIRE OF JUSTINIAN IN SPITE OF ITS SUPERFICIAL strength was economically insecure. Great as was the public revenue it barely balanced the huge expenditure on public works, the salaries due to so large a civil service, the subsidies paid to subject allies, the upkeep of a fleet and army. There is frequent evidence of arrears but none of a reserve. Taxation was no longer excessive in the towns. The Emperor Anastasius had given fresh incentives to the merchants by abolishing the profit tax, the *chrysargyron*. But agriculture was being sapped by the coincidence of land tax and capitation tax, while the custom of extorting contributions in kind and forced labour from the peasants and the town proletariat must have made many of them welcome any alternative to the Imperial tax gatherer.

It seems likely that the Imperial authority was regarded as inevitable in the Eastern provinces, but if it were to be challenged there would be no religious or cultural unity adequate for its support. There is evidence that the worship of the old gods was still a vital force until the 7th century. The Christians had been bitterly divided by the 5th-century controversies as to the nature of the Incarnation. These divisions had early become associated with the rivalry between the two political factions, 'The Blues' and 'The Greens'; by the early 6th century they were becoming linked with different linguistic and racial groupings. By the end of the 6th century the native-speaking populations in Egypt, in Syria and in Armenia were all vehemently opposed to the religious policy of Constantinople.

This last development was the more ominous since from the middle of the 5th century there had been a marked resurgence of Syriac culture in Syria and of Coptic culture in Egypt; both had come to possess their own literature and art-forms. Armenia had always been distinct.

It might have seemed that the Empire would collapse in the first crises brought about by serious external pressure: it almost did so. In the year 602 the Emperor Maurice was killed by his mutinous troops as he was attempting to check the Slav hordes pressing south across the Danube. The Persians under Khusru II broke the eastern frontier, conquered Egypt, Syria and Palestine, ravaged Asia Minor and threatened Constantinople. When at last the Persians had been defeated in 629 by the Emperor Heraclius there was a new threat from the south. The Arabs had been united by the preaching of Islam. Muhammad had died in 632 but by 635 his followers had conquered Syria, by 638 Palestine and by 642 Egypt. By 670 the Arabs were over-running North Africa, by 673 they were besieging Constanti-nople. They were checked there and driven from Asia Minor, but they returned and Constantinople nearly fell to them in the siege of 717. The crisis was probably over by 750 but it was not until the accession of Michael II in 820 that the Empire could be judged to be secure. Perhaps the chief factor in its survival had been the retention of Asia Minor, since this made it both economically and militarily viable.

The years between 602 and 840 are still the most obscure and unexplored in the history of Byzantine art. But they include the crucial disputes on the meaning of an ikon.

The Byzantine conception of the function of the Christian image had finally developed by the year 787. At the time of the accession of Anastasius it was an immemorial custom to decorate the walls and sometimes the roof and floors of Christian churches, baptisteries and funerary chambers. But the purpose of these wall-paintings and mosaics had been conceived either as purely decorative or as primarily didactic; through the use of symbols and of narrative scenes the Christian could be taught the mysteries of the faith or could contemplate them. There is no evidence that images were either prayed to or prayed through; and it was only gradually that they were venerated.

It is sometimes asserted that the emergence of the Christian cult image in the late 5th and 6th centuries was due to pagan religious influences which had been brought into Christianity through mass conversions. This has never been substantiated. It is of course very possible that this was a factor in the devotions of the illiterate, particularly among the proletariat of the great Eastern cities. But the Christian episcopate and priesthood and educated laity seem to have been singularly immune from direct pagan religious influences, for behind them lay centuries of bitter anti-pagan polemic often directed against image-worship.[1] In contrast by the late 4th century they were very ready to receive secular influences from the non-Christian Graeco-Roman world. Two such influences directly stimulated the new development. They were the veneration of the Imperial Image and the use of funerary portraits.

It had long been held that there was a special relationship between the Emperor and his Image. Its presence signified his presence by proxy, any honour or insult paid to it was paid to him. By natural association such a conception could be transferred from official secular art to the art of the new official religion. Increasingly Christ was shown in the apse to signify that He presided at the altar beneath Him. The presence of the angels and saints sharing in the liturgy was signified by their representations as they hovered above the altar or moved processionally towards it. If the image was conceived present as a proxy, honour paid it would pass to the Imaged.[2]

The fact that this conception was derived from official secular art, not from religious, would make it acceptable in the

Christian Church; but it would remain intelligible to any civil servant, even when he was only nominally a Christian, for it had received classic expression in the writings of Porphyry and Julian. Towards the end of the 3rd century Porphyry had noted 'if someone makes a portrait of a friend he does not believe the friend himself to be in it, nor that the limbs of his body are confined within the parts of the painting, but that the respect for the friend is shown through the portrait'.[3] Julian wrote 'we do not say that the statues of the emperors are mere wood and stone and bronze, nor that they are the emperors themselves, but that they are images of the emperors. He therefore who loves the Emperor delights to see the emperor's statue.' 'It follows that he who loves the gods delights to gaze on the images of the gods and their likenesses, and he feels reverence and shudders in awe of the gods who look at him from the unseen world.'[4]

Such an attitude was conventional among educated men and to be ignorant of it was held to be the mark of the illiterate. A fragment of a treatise by Porphyry on Images has been preserved in the third book of the *Praeparatio Evangelica* of Eusebius of Caesarea. 'The utterly unlearned regard statues as wood and stone, just as those who do not understand written letters look upon monuments as stones and on tablets as bits of wood and on books as woven papyrus.'

But to those who whether Christian or non-Christian had been affected by Middle Platonism an image could either be the representation of the visible or of the invisible, a shadow of the visible or a materialization of the invisible. In the latter case its meaning might only become clear to the initiate. The same fragment by Porphyry begins 'I speak to those who lawfully may hear. Depart all ye profane and close the doors. I will show to those who have learned to read from the statues as from books the things there written concerning the gods, the thoughts of a wise theology wherein man indicated God and Divine Powers by images akin to sense and sketched invisible things in visible forms.'[5]

Such a conception of the function of religious images could be absorbed easily into Early Byzantine Christian thought with its Middle Platonist undertones. But though it is clear that under Justinian the Sacred Images were venerated and contemplated there is no evidence that they were in any sense worshipped or invoked among the educated;[6] writing about 540 in his *De Opificio Mundi* (VI, 10) John Philoponos considers it a characteristically pagan tenet that worship paid to an image could be referred to God.

But there had been a parallel development in popular Christianity which had led to the conception of a wonder-working ikon which should be touched and could be prayed through. By the 6th century portable panel-paintings of saints would seem to have been in common use, kept in private houses or placed at cross-roads or in wayside shrines. A number from this period were preserved in the monastery of St Katherine on Sinai, where the earliest of them seem late 5th century. They are wooden tablets. The heads painted on them in encaustic wax are full-faced, motionless and conventionalized and are obviously derived directly from the secular funerary portraits of the non-Christian period, so many examples of which have survived from Roman Egypt. There is evidence that they were used in private devotions and some were reputed to work miracles. But it should be noted that wonder-working Images of this period belong to two categories. Some were held to be of directly miraculous origin—'images not made with hands'; others contained 'the sacred dust'. It would seem therefore that they were held to work miracles not as images but as relics.[7] The miraculous power was held to pass through physical contact. 'The

14 CHRIST ENTHRONED AMONG HIS APOSTLES

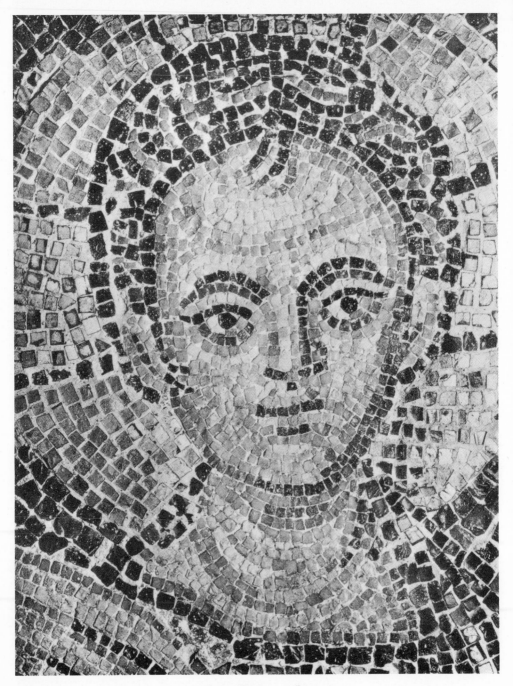

15　THE CHILD CHRIST

image not made with hands' would seem normally to have been created by some physical contact with the Original,[8] like the impression of the Face upon the cloth. The image of the sacred dust contained something of the body of the original, like the sweat scraped from a stylite saint. It was for this reason that the wonder-working ikon was touched as well as prayed before.

Just as the cult of martyrs gave impetus to the cult of relics, the cult of relics gave impetus to the cult of ikons. Its growth was also fostered by the increasing strength of the cult of the Mother of God, of the Angels, and of Saints, and of the emphasis on personal links with heavenly patrons.

The few fragments of 7th-century Byzantine art that survived the destruction by the Iconoclasts[9] suggest that there was an increasing emphasis on the isolated figure or the dominant figure presented frontally, perhaps the better to be invoked. There is some evidence towards the end of the century of a tendency against symbolism. In 692 the Trullan Council decreed in its eighty-second canon: 'in order that perfection be represented before all peoples even in paintings, we ordain from now on that the human figure of Christ our God, the Lamb, who took on the sins of the world, be set up even in the images instead of the ancient lamb. Through this figure we realize the height of the humiliation of God the Word and are led to remember His life in the flesh, His suffering and His saving death and the redemption ensuing from it for the world.'[10]

The Byzantine veneration of images reached its height at the beginning of the 8th century in the Eastern seaport towns and at the shrines of the great abbeys. There was an inevitable reaction. In 730 the Emperor Leo III, the Isaurian, issued an Edict that decreed the destruction of all images in human form of Christ and of His Mother and of His saints and angels. This was the

beginning of the struggle between Iconoclast and Iconodule—
image-destroyers and image-worshippers—which divided Byzantine Christianity for a hundred and thirteen years.

The origins and the character of Iconoclasm have been
frequently misrepresented—in the first place by the Iconodules.
It is still sometimes ascribed to Muslim influence and the fear of
the graven image. But the Iconoclast emperors were munificent
patrons of art who delighted in graven images. It has been
described as puritanical, but the Iconoclasts luxuriously em-
bellished their churches; the Cross that represented Christ, like
the Peacocks that stood for immortality and the Trees for
Paradise, was placed against wide backgrounds of gold mosaic
and interspersed with purely decorative compositions. Iconoclasm has been attributed to the personal convictions of Leo III,
but it would seem that he was hesitantly following a movement
begun by a group of bishops in Asia Minor; it is very improbable
that he would have done so if Iconoclasm had not been supported
by his army, mainly recruited from the conservative Christian
peasantry of the Asia Minor uplands.

The central tenet of Iconoclasm was that all corporeal images
must be removed from places of worship since their presence
there led to idolatry. In some cases this may have been correct—
we know a little about the popular superstitions of the city
proletariat.[11] On the same grounds there was at times some
Iconoclast hostility to the practice of invocation, though this is
commonly overstressed.[12] Still, no literate Iconodule however
extreme would ever have defended any form of idolatry. Both
sides appealed to the orthodox Christology of the Chalcedon
Council. Fundamentally the dispute was not a doctrinal one.

Between 741 and 775, during the reign of the second Iconoclast Emperor Constantine V, the movement came to be supported by those who wished that the monks of each diocese

should be under the effective control of their bishops. It therefore came to be supported by the mass of the episcopate. In 754
three hundred and thirty-eight bishops declared for Iconoclasm
at the Council of Hiereia. But it also had the support of all those
who wished the Church to be under the effective control of the
Emperor and these must have formed an influential section of the
administration. In contrast and perhaps partly in consequence
the Iconodule opposition was led by the great majority of the
monks and by all those who like St Theodore the Studite cared
deeply for the freedom of the Church. It is thus easy to understand that Iconoclasm was supported by some very moderate
Iconoclasts and 'image-worship' by some very moderate Iconodules. But it is also probable that neither the extreme Iconoclasts
nor the extreme Iconodules were as extreme as their opponents
suggested.

The acrimony and the duration of the controversy upon the
Images only becomes intelligible if it was in reality also a struggle
between two political factions and if it had its roots not in that
complete fantasy 'a Semitic horror of the image' but in socio-
logical and therefore ultimately in economic factors.

The political and economic turmoil of the 7th and 8th
centuries had led to a reorganization of the political and social
structure of the Byzantine Empire which seems to have begun
under Heraclius (610–641) and to have been consummated under
Leo III (717–741). The Imperial government developed a consistent policy of fostering a free peasantry since Imperial estates
were divided among peasant holders who were obliged to per-
form military services. The guilds were still more closely
organized in the towns and prices strictly controlled. The
ancient provinces, the Dioceses, were regrouped and normally
subdivided into Themes, each under the effective military control
of a *strategos*. The powers of the great ministers were curtailed:

there was no longer a Master of the Offices and three officials shared the authority once held by the Prefect of the Sacred Chamber.

It is tenable that the Iconoclast party was the party of Leo III and Constantine V, who held to this policy in its entirety, and that the Iconodule party represented the shifting elements of a conservative opposition. This would explain why the strength of the Iconoclasts lay with the army recruited from the peasant freeholders and how the Iconodule Empress Irene was raised to power by a strong faction of the civil service among the acclamations of the city proletariat. It would be characteristically East Roman that two political parties or affinities should have distinguished themselves, sincerely enough, by a doctrinal badge just as in the late 5th and early 6th centuries the Faction of the Blues had been linked with the Chalcedonians and the Faction of the Greens with the Monophysites.

This theory does not deny a religious element in the Iconoclast controversy but suggests that it has commonly been over-estimated. It is significant that in reverses neither side clung to their religious opinions with the pertinacity shown earlier by the Monophysites. Theodore of Studios describes the Iconodule collapse when the Iconoclast party came back into power at the accession of Leo V. 'Almost every soul yielded and gave his signature to the impious. Few offer resistance and they are tested by misfortune as by fire. Among the bishops there backslid he of Smyrna and he of Cherson; among the Abbots he of Chrysopolis, he of Dios, he of Chora and almost all those in the city; ... of the lay order nobody holds his ground except Peximenites, and he has been beaten and exiled; among the clerics the admirable Gregory who is nicknamed Kentrokukuros; from among the Abbesses six at the most and they are guarded in nunneries.'[13] Similarly the Iconoclasm still dominant under the

Emperor Theophilus (829–842) seems to vanish when he was succeeded by Michael III. Perhaps it vanished so completely because the Iconodule emperors of the Amorian and Macedonian house carried out so many of the policies of their Iconoclast predecessors. Perhaps the controversy ended not in a religious compromise but in a social and political one.

On such an interpretation the Iconoclast-Iconodule controversy was only superficially concerned with Sacred Images. But the polemics to which it gave rise led to a new precision in the Byzantine conception of their function.

On the 13th of October 787, when the Iconodule party was in power under the Empress Irene and her young son Constantine VI, a definition upon sacred ikons was drawn up at the seventh session of the ecumenical Second Council of Nicea. Nine days later it was promulgated at the Magnaura palace in the Imperial presence. Its binding and ecumenical authority was reasserted in 843 at the Council of Constantinople. From then its authority was to remain unquestioned and it marks the final development of the Byzantine conception of the Image. It reads: 'We define with all accuracy and care that the venerable and holy ikons be set up like the form of the venerable and life-giving Cross, inasmuch as matter consisting of colours and of small stones and of other material is appropriate in the holy church of God, on sacred vessels and on vestments, on walls, on panels, in houses and on roads; both the image of our Lord and God and Saviour Jesus Christ and that of our undefiled Lady the Holy Mother of God and those of the Angels-worthy-of-honour and those of all holy and pious men. For the more frequently they are seen by means of painted representation the more those who behold them are aroused to remember and to desire the prototypes and to give them greeting and worship-of-honour, but not the true worship of our faith which befits only the Divine

Nature; and to offer to them both incense and candles in the same way as to the shape of the venerable and life-giving Cross and to the holy books of the Evangel and to other sacred objects, as was the custom even of the ancients.'[14]

After 843 this Decree was interpreted in the light of the teaching of the chief Iconodule controversialist St John of Damascus, the Damascene, and his doctrine became official. It was far more moderate than the views attributed by Iconoclasts or by modern scholars. It is still stated authoritatively that the picture was considered to be 'a magical counterpart of the prototype and has a magical identity with it'.[15] But I cannot trace either idea earlier than to Dr Holl in 1907. An image was no more conceived to be identical with the Imaged than a man's shadow is conceived as being identical with a man. It is repeatedly emphasized that the image differs from the Imaged according to its very nature, its *ousia*.[16] Sacred Images were to be honoured but it is expressly forbidden by the Decree to give them true worship. To the Damascene it is the height of madness and impiety to attempt to make an image of the godhead[17] which is by nature infinite. Angels can be imaged because though invisible they are finite.[18] He held that no veneration or honour should be paid to the image as an object,[19] as an object it is simply a piece of matter; the honour is paid to the prototype it represents and even that honour must not be more than simple *proskynesis*,[20] the same honour that is paid to relics, to consecrated things and to men worthy of respect.[21] An image is a silent sermon,[22] it is the book of the illiterate,[23] it is a memorial of the mysteries of God.[24]

All this seems very far from the conception of the image as a magical counterpart, but the Damascene also considers the image as a channel through which strength can pass to us as well as knowledge. 'While living the saints were filled by the Holy

Spirit, and after death the grace of the Holy Spirit is never far from their souls, nor from their bodies in their tombs, nor from their holy images.'[25] The two factors in the development of the conception of the Sacred Image, its association with the martyr's relic and with the Imperial portrait, had blended.

In 787 at the first session of the Second Council of Nicea the Bishop Theodosius had stated 'if the Imperial effigies are sent through the cities and the provinces, the crowd comes to meet them bearing wax tapers and incense, thus honouring not a picture painted in wax but the Emperor; how much more then should this happen to the image of Christ our God painted in the Church, of his unstained Mother and of all the Saints, both Blessed Fathers and Ascetics'.[26]

Honour passed through the image to the Imaged just as honour passed through the Imperial effigy to the Emperor. Strength passed from the Imaged through the image just as healing could pass from the Saint through his relic. The sacred ikon was not identical with its prototype but by the middle of the 9th century it had become a part of orthodoxy that it could be a channel to it and from it and as a reflection signify its presence.

The conception of the 'wonder-working ikon' had thus been officially authorized, and now it could be the occasion of miracles not as a relic but as an image; standing beneath it the believer could be healed as the Saint's shadow fell upon him. Again, just as man's presence can be argued from the presence of his shadow, so the presence of the God-Bearer and the Saint were in some fashion reflected by that of their images.[27] This led to localized cults, notably of the Mother of God[28] and created the classic scheme of Byzantine church decoration.

For the Byzantine Church was turning into a single great ikon. It has been suggested from the literary evidence that the

6th-century attitude to church architecture was prosaic enough. But by the end of the 9th century there is an underlying symbolism.[29] The church is a microcosm representing all earth and sky. The Eucharist was at the heart of the church like the Passion at the heart of the world. Christ and His Mother and the Angels were present through their images in the dome and in the high vaults and in the conch of the apse: the sky of the church, the Kingdom of Heaven. On the lower half of the walls Saints moved among the Church militant on earth. The intermediate sphere was the link between man's life on earth and the Kingdom of Heaven; it was therefore the natural setting for the Gospel narrative. Scenes from the New Testament and from the New Testament Apocrypha were present here through the mosaics and paintings that were their shadows.

This scheme was to be obscured in the late medieval period through the custom of placing wooden panels of Christ and His Mother beneath their sky representations for them to be touched, and through the desire to represent an increasing number both of Saints and of Feasts.

But at least from the 9th to the late 11th century the church could be conceived as a threefold ikon, with the triple interpretation which is recurrent through Byzantine symbolism and which is ultimately linked with the multiple senses of Scripture. A church is not only a representation of the whole world, it also represents the setting of Christ's life on earth,[30] so that the conch of the apse is an image of the cave of Bethlehem, the altar that of the table of the Last Supper, the ciborium above it is the sepulchre. Again a church is an image of the liturgical year[31] and the lesser images within it follow the sequence of the yearly liturgy. Meditating on the scenes that represented the Twelve or sometimes Fifteen Mysteries that began with the Annunciation and ended with the close of the Virgin's life on earth, the believer could feel himself present in turn at each in chronologic order.

This threefold inner meaning of the church was based on the literal fact that it was a building in which the Mystery was held to be re-enacted, also literally.

Once a church was conceived as itself an image the relationship between religious art and architecture grew close to the point of fusion. Both gain their meaning from the liturgy and the form of presentation of mosaics became determined by the use to which they might be put by worshippers within the building. This seems a rather different ideal from the *kosmesis* of Justinian with its primary object that the church should appear beautiful.

Praying before the holy images men now prayed through them as channels and so reached their prototypes. This led to the final victory of frontality; only those figures with which the worshipper would wish to make no contact are shown in profile —like Judas at the Betrayal.[32] When the representation of the full face was scenically impossible the three-quarter view was predominant.[33] The new optical contrivances of the Macedonian period were aimed to emphasize or to facilitate a personal link between the image and the believer.

9

Amorians and Macedonians

THE FINAL DEVELOPMENT OF THE SACRED IMAGE HAD had effect on the practice of Byzantine art. The last, more dialectic phase of anti-Iconoclast polemic had also provided new elements in Byzantine art theory through the analysis of the function of the *phantasia*, through the claim for the priority of sight among the senses and through the conception of the four-fold causality of a painting. But these are perhaps best discussed after an attempt to reconstruct the Amorian and Macedonian Age.

Two family groupings, those of the Amorians and of the Macedonians, held the Imperial throne from 820 to 1056; perhaps they were in fact only one. Eudoxia Ingerina, the wife of Basil the first Macedonian (867–886) had also been the mistress of Michael III the last Amorian (842–867). Leo VI the Wise (886–912), though legally the son of Basil, may well have been the son of Michael and there is some evidence that this was a conception that he fostered.

A mark of this phase of Byzantine history was the emphasis on family continuity as a symbol of continuity in Imperial policy. The Macedonians were not a dynasty in the Western sense, they were a family network like that which had provided the Julio-Claudian Principate at the birth of the Empire. Emperors who did not belong to it by birth joined it through marriage alliances, as did Romanos I Lekapenos (919–944), who made himself the father-in-law of his Macedonian ward Constantine VIII; or Nikephoros II Phokas (963–969), who married the Empress Theophano, widow of the Macedonian Romanos II (959–963); or again Michael IV (1034–1041) and Constantine IX Mono-machos (1042–1055) who had married the Macedonian princess Zoe.

Such family contacts emphasized the identity of the Imperial administration. The Byzantine Empire of this period was different in three ways from that of Justinian. It was far smaller in extent; it essentially consisted of Greece, part of the South Balkans, Thrace and Asia Minor, with footholds in South Italy and the Caucasus, though it was gradually to expand into Northern Syria and Northern Mesopotamia. Partly as a result, it had become culturally and linguistically homogeneous. The Coptic- and Syriac-speaking peasants and traders were now under Arab rule. Armenia was most often a border State. The Byzantines still called themselves Romans, *Romaioi*; but Greek, either in its literary or in its popular forms, was the universal language of the Empire. Latin, which had been the official language of Justinian, had vanished leaving only a mass of loan words. The Empire had also become homogeneous in religion. Popular paganism was being absorbed into the popular beliefs of a Christian peasantry. Educated crypto-paganism had faded into a nostalgic literary tendency and an occasional practical interest in demonology. The dispute as to the nature of the Incarnation had closed with the final victory of the Chalcedonians. The debate as to the use of religious images was ending in the victory of the moderate Iconodules. All citizens accepted the single orthodoxy of a universal Church.

It has been customary to speak of Byzantine Caesaro-Papism but that seems an anachronism—perhaps the result of reading back into a Byzantine past the half-Lutheran Church and State practice of the later tsars. The Sacred Emperor might be conceived as the Moses of his people; the Patriarch of Con-stantinople was their Aaron. The doctrines and the moral teach-ings of the Church could no more be changed by either than the laws of geometry. Spiritual and secular administration were distinct as two functions in a single organism. The prestige of the Apostolic See of St Peter at Rome was very high and on occasion its authority was appealed to; a brief uneasy quarrel between Rome and Constantinople when Photios was Patriarch was followed by a long uneasy peace. But as a whole the Byzantines of this period tended to be oblivious of the barbarian West. Theirs was a civilization and an empire that turned inwards on itself. To them Constantinople was the centre of the world.[1]

Although the Empire under the Macedonians was homogeneously Orthodox, it is, I think, a common mistake to over-emphasize the essentially religious character of its culture and therefore of its art. There is evidence for the vivid strength of popular Christianity and it was the great age of monastic foundations—Mount Athos is a 10th-century creation. But the Imperial administration still provided the patronage for fine art and this was perhaps rather aloof from the manifestations of popular devotion even if on occasion it utilized them.

A passage from the *Philopatris* (963–969) describes a visit to a monastery. It would be impossible to find any early medieval Western counterpart either in its attitude to the abbey inmates or in the pervasive echoes from the classics. 'An old man with the grim look of a Titan plucked me by the sleeve and said he had been initiated by them into all the mysteries, so we went through iron gates and over floors of bronze and climbing round and round the many steps of a staircase we came to a house with a roof of gold like the house of Menelaus that Homer describes. I gazed at everything much as did the young man from the island (Telemachus from Ithaka). But I did not see Helen; I saw only some stooping and pallid-faced men. When they caught sight of us they rejoiced and came to meet us asking us: Did we bring any bad news? By their looks they seemed as if they hoped for the worst and took pleasure in misfortunes like the Furies on the stage.'[2]

Becoming culturally homogeneous the Byzantine Empire had become far more effectively a corporate State. Each branch of industry was a corporation with its own monopoly but subject to a State control which determined not only the profits of its members but the conditions of their admission. Imperial factories monopolized not only the production of armaments but that of articles of luxury. All quarries, mines and saltpans like all caravanserais were the property of the Emperor. It has been calculated that the annual State revenue exceeded, perhaps greatly exceeded, one hundred million gold francs.[3] The Purse had become part of the Imperial insignia and the Emperor Nikephoros Phokas threatened that with his gold he could shatter the 'Empire' of the West as if it were an earthen vessel. Constantinople, through the loss of Egypt and of Syria to the Arabs, became the successor city to Alexandria and to Antioch as well as to Rome. It was also the predecessor of Venice as the chief *entrepôt* for Eastern trade. It was never to be so wealthy or so thickly populated as in the 9th and 10th centuries.

The length of the reigns of successful emperors must have deepened the sense of security. There were no greater rulers, different as each was from the other, than Basil I, Leo VI the Wise and Constantine VII Porphyrogenitos; together they cover the years from 867 to 959. The great Basil II the Bulgar Slayer was to reign from 976 to 1025. It is only after 1025 that the economic and therefore social structure became so oddly and so rapidly undermined.

Looking back on this creative phase in the history of Byzantine art and architecture it seems to be in sharp contrast to its contemporary phase in Byzantine literature. The literature is barren, partly because of the value placed on an encyclopaedic approach to the Greek classics as in the case of Photios, partly because of a standard of impeccable but frozen good taste that could be illustrated by the poems of John Geometres and Cometas the Cartularius. There was no original speculation primarily because a group of earlier Greek philosophers and theologians[4] had been elected to form a Canon of Fathers and it had become the principal duty of the Christian author to select and to arrange the truths they had enunciated. It was an age of anthologists. The *Palatine Anthology* of Greek epigrams[5] has been its characteristic legacy to European literature.

Yet once again the inventiveness that would have made a scholar suspect was valued in applied mathematics. There is evidence for experiments in logistics and geodesy. The new achievements in Macedonian architecture are those of applied geometry.

The New Church, the Nea, founded at Constantinople by the Emperor Basil I was the Haghia Sophia of that age. An equal-armed cross was inscribed within a circle, a dome was placed at the point of intersection of the two straight lines of the cross, four others were placed at the corners. With its many domes, diminishing vaults and decorated façades it was to be the fore-runner of a new type of Byzantine architecture of which St Mark's at Venice is a variant. The straight line was beginning to be found monotonous—a monotony relieved by fresh architectural experiments and by the avoidance of the derivatives from the basilica plan. A zest for elegance had led to a distaste for the massive; slim columns take the place of piers as a support for domes. The blank external walls were replaced by façades covered with elaborate geometric patterns which are emphasized by changes of colour: red brick alternates with white rubble, glazed earthen bowls and glazed tiles are inserted to represent the circle and the square.

If the inventiveness of the geometrician architects was clearly prized so too was the ingenuity of the craftsmen that they employed. The period of the Amorian and Macedonian emperors is essentially that of 'the working of wonders', the *thaumatopoiike*; there was a delight in mechanical contrivances which were often only elaborate mechanical toys of precious material. Like so much else in this phase of Byzantine history the fashion probably developed during the almost unexplored reign of Theophilus (829–842) though the classic account of such wonders dates from the autumn of 949 when Liutprand, Bishop of Cremona, was received by the Emperor in the Magnaura palace at Constantinople. He writes: 'A tree made of brass but gilded over stood before the Emperor's throne. The boughs were full of birds of different kinds, also made of brass and also gilt, which sang in a chorus of different birdsongs according to their kind. The Emperor's throne was constructed with such skill that at one time it was level with the ground, at another it was raised above it and then in a moment it hung aloft. It was guarded as it were by lions of immense size—one could not be sure if they were made of brass or wood but they were certainly covered with gold on the surface—which opening their mouths and moving their tongues roared aloud and shook the ground with their tails. Here I was brought into the presence of the Emperor supported on the shoulders of two eunuchs. The lions roared at my coming and the birds sang according to their kind. Thrice I performed the act of adoration prone at full length upon the ground. Then I raised my head. Behold, the Emperor whom I had just before seen seated almost on the level of the ground now appeared to my eyes dressed in different robes almost level with the ceiling of the palace.'[6]

But though inventiveness in architects and ingenuity in their craftsmen were both valued no man could achieve the prestige of a savant by his novelties. In this period there seems to have been a slight shift downwards in the social structure both for architects and for artists.[7] There is no Macedonian parallel to the position accorded to Anthemius or the two Isidores; the greatest of the Macedonian architects are anonymous. The artists and craftsmen rank as *ergolaboi*—men who work by contract on materials provided for them by their employers and are paid partly in advance. The twenty-second chapter of the *Book of the Eparch* describes their place in Byzantine social organization; it most probably dates from the reign of Leo the Wise (886–912). It is entitled 'concerning all *ergolaboi* or joiners, plasterers, stone-masons, locksmiths, painters and the like'.[8]

The first section describes their rather restricted rights: 'Craftsmen who make a contract for any job and receive an advance upon it are not to leave that job and undertake another unless they have finally completed the job. But if through lack of materials or owing to some misconduct of the man who gives the job there should be a delay, the proper materials not being furnished to the craftsman for the completion of the job, then the craftsman whatever his craft may be shall signify the same to the giver of the job with due notice or attestation; and if (the employer) is responsible for the delay an appeal should be made to the Prefect, and then the craftsman may, with his sanction, start another job.'

The second section deals with the penalties to which they are subject: 'Should the aforesaid *ergolaboi* from greed or from malice prepense leave the job which they have undertaken and take on another job, it shall be lawful for the giver of the job to notify them in the presence of witnesses, reminding them in such notice of the agreement as set out in writing or made by word of mouth. . . . Craftsmen who have disregarded the agreement which they have made shall be brought to reason by flogging, mutilation and deportation.'

The third section refers to the failings of the 'craftsmen who

16 THE IMPERIAL HOMAGE
[*pp. 16, 124*]

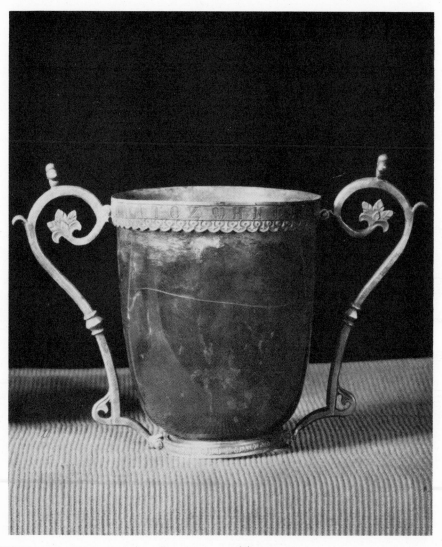

17   LINE AND TEXTURE

aim at getting a number of jobs, with the result that they are distracted by having them all on their hands, or who now cheat one employer and now mislead another, or who, as sometimes happens, use glib talk and awkward behaviour as tricks to increase their earnings'.

There is some evidence for a slight rise in status in the late 10th and early 11th century. In the *Menologion* of Basil II (976–1025) there are eight signatures of illuminators; British Museum Additional MS. 19352 contains the statement that it was written and illuminated by Theodoros of Caesarea 'in the year 6574' (1066).[9] It seems likely that under the Amorian and Macedonian emperors there was an even sharper contrast between the position of the scholar and the artist than at any other period of Byzantine social history.

Yet in contrast a picture was never valued so highly in any other phase of the unbroken Greek tradition. This was partly the result of the development of the theory of the *phantasia*, partly to the Iconodule theory of the priority of sight among the five senses, partly to the consequent conception of a picture not only as *graphe* but as *logos*, a writing and a word. For the 8th-century Byzantine *phantasia* was something at once more limited and more essential than Imagination. It was the necessary prolegomenon to the faculty of *aisthesis*; it was the receptacle on which sense images were impressed and in which they were received and stored.

This gave a fresh depth to Greek art criticism, for though the achievements of archaic and classical Greek art were unsurpassed it may be suggested tentatively that the aesthetic theory accompanying them was rather jejune. Much of it seems to be summarized by Aristotle in the *Poetics* in a passage that must have been familiar to many Byzantine scholars after the Aristotelian revival that is associated with Leontius of Byzantium: 'The reason why people enjoy seeing pictures is that the spectators learn and infer what each object is—this, they say, is so-and-so; while if one has not seen the thing before, the pleasure is produced not by the imitation but by the execution, the colour, or some such cause.'[10]

Many classical Greek poems have survived, composed in praise of works of art; but these are praised for their deceptive resemblance to nature, so that a live calf comes to suck from the udders of Myron's heifer or birds peck at the grapes of Zeuxis. Even the poem on the pictures of Parhasius, attributed to the painter and so much admired as art criticism, does nothing more than state the necessary limitations of imitation, *mimesis*: 'I affirm that the clear limits of this art have been found under my hand and the mark is fixed fast that cannot be exceeded, though nothing mortal is flawless.'[11]

It is not until the 3rd century A.D. with the *Enneads* of Plotinus that there is any conception of an art which could be closer to reality than is nature. It has been suggested that such an aesthetic theory could explain many of the primary achievements both of archaic and Byzantine art, but for Byzantine scholars Plotinus was primarily an echo caught in Proclus; he had none of the authority of 'golden-tongued Plato', who had taught in the *Republic* that the graphic arts were trebly removed from reality since they were employed to make semblances of external objects which are themselves only the shadows of the truth.[12]

Professor J. W. Mackail wrote: 'Aristotle does indeed in one often quoted passage assign to poetry a higher truth and a deeper seriousness than that of actual things. But not until the Byzantine period do we find this clearly laid down as a property of the other fine arts. Nilus Scholasticus, a Christian epigrammatist of the 5th century, speaks of the office of a picture being to bring up its object into "intellectual memory". The phrase is harsh and scholastic; but the thought it implies is the necessary antecedent of the remarkable verses of Agathias on the picture of the fawn which have the very tone and spirit of "The Ode on a Grecian Urn".'[13]

Perhaps Professor Mackail slightly overstated the case. In the 6th century Nilus the Scholastic wrote upon a painting of an Angel, 'how daring it is to give shape to the bodiless, yet the image leads us up to the intellectual memory of heavenly beings';[14] the image imprinting itself on the *phantasia* like a seal reawakens earlier, perhaps pre-natal, memories. A similar conception of the image imprinting itself on the *phantasia* as on wax seems implicit in the line by Agathias, 'gazing, he imprints the image within himself'.[15] The poem in the *Planudean Appendix* by Agathias to which Professor Mackail referred can be understood as the interpretation of a scene impressed on the *phantasia*.[16]

Yet the Byzantine conception of the relation of the *phantasia* to the impact of a picture seems to have been first formulated in the 9th century as a result of the Iconoclast controversy. Behind it lay two statements in the third chapter of the third book of the *De Anima* of Aristotle, '*phantasia* is the faculty by virtue of which we say that an image presents itself to us'.[17] '*Phantasia* has derived even its name from light (*phaos*) because without light one cannot see.'[18] St Theodore the Studite, who died in 826, writes to Naukratios[19] that the soul possesses five faculties: *phantasia*, *aisthesis*, *doxa*, *dianoia*, *nous*; the last four depend upon *phantasia* and for this reason he defends the use of ikons. It is a difficult passage. In the *Parva Catechesis*[20] Theodore asserts that the soul only possesses three faculties and it seems likely therefore that he linked together *phantasia-aisthesis* and *doxa-dianoia* and saw them culminating in *nous*; imagination and sense perception leading to judgement, judgement leading to the final act of mind.

On this reading *phantasia* has become the part of *aisthesis* by which a pictorial image is reflected and in which it remains stored: imagination as the source of memory.

St John of Damascus wrote in the twentieth chapter of the second book of the *Exposition of the Orthodox Faith*: 'The faculty of imagination, having apprehended material objects through the senses, transmits this to the faculty of thought or reason—for they are both the same—and this, having passed judgement on it, passes it on to the faculty of memory. Now the organ of memory is the hindmost ventricle of the brain and the vital spirit it contains.'[21] For the Damascene *phantasia* and *aisthesis* is either essentially one or if distinguished are two parts of a single power. Three chapters earlier he had written, 'Imagination is a faculty of the unreasoning part of the soul. It is through the organs of sense that it is brought into action and it is spoken of as sensation, . . . sensation is that faculty of the soul whereby material objects can be apprehended or discriminated, . . . the sense of sight is the visual faculty but the object of sight is that which comes within the scope of the sense of sight. . . . It is to be observed that sight is possible only in straight lines.'[22]

Sight was now conceived as the queen of the senses; it functioned through the presence of light, its objects were colours; forms were perceived by their colour differentiations. St John of Damascus died about 750, but by the middle of the 9th century his writings had been placed in the Canon of the Fathers and possessed an unchallengeable authority. He stated, 'the first sense is sight and the organs of sight are the nerves of the brain and the eyes. Now sight is primarily the perception of colour; with the colour, it discriminates the body that has colour and its size and its shape and its placing and the intervening space and the number.'[23] It was natural that Iconodule controversialists should emphasize the primacy of sight over hearing.

Sometime between 820 and 828 Nikephoros of Constantinople wrote in his *Refutatio et Eversio*, 'For we all know that sight is the most honoured and the most necessary of the senses, and that it may allow a more distinct and sharp apprehension of what falls under perception; for it is the nature of that which is heard to travel less quickly than that which is seen. Seeing will attract faster than the other senses since it has attractive power to a greater degree.'[24] In a passage in his *Apologeticus Maior* Nikephoros had already taught that the sense of sight produces more durable impressions than the sense of hearing[25]—perhaps this is because they are stored in the *phantasia*.

Under the Amorians and Macedonians, Byzantine aesthetic theory seems to have placed all its emphasis on sight and on the colours—and therefore forms—sight apprehended. This is a contrast to the 4th-century Cappadocian school with their emphasis on the power of the word and the delights of poetry, or to the analogies from music that had been drawn by Proclus and by Pseudo-Dionysius. The sense of hearing was treated very cursorily by the Damascene; 'it is that whereby voices and sounds are perceived, and it distinguishes these as sharp or deep or smooth or loud. Its organs are the soft nerves of the brain and the structure of the ears. Man and the ape are the only animals that do not move their ears.'[26]

It seems odd therefore that the painter was not accorded the position previously held by the rhetorician and the poet. Perhaps this was due to the conception of the nature of the causality which produced the picture or the mosaic. In his second *Antirrhetikos* Nikephoros describes in detail how a picture comes into being.[27] An artist paints either on a panel or on a wall. He uses either pigments or pebbles (mosaic tessellae). The subject of his painting need not be present. The bodily outline of the subject is moulded by painting. The painting then has a separate existence from its subject but is related to it as to its prototype, its *paradeigma*. In Aristotelian terminology the subject of the painting is its formal cause and the formal cause matters far more than the efficient cause that was the painter.

This passage seems to provide a clue to the fivefold causality of a picture described in the *Refutatio et Eversio*.[28] Here Nikephoros refers to the fact that every ikon has five causes; the poetic, the organic, the formal, the material and the final. The classification must be derived (probably through a handbook) from the fourfold causality analysed in Book Delta of the *Metaphysics*. The problem is not what was intended by Aristotle but how it was interpreted by 9th-century Byzantines.

The material cause is not only 'the pigments and the pebbles' referred to by Nikephoros out of which the image is made, but the materials which have produced these colour effects and these tessellae; the more glorious the subject of the image the more precious should be the materials employed in it.

The meaning of the two efficient causes of a work of art, 'the poetic' and 'the organic' of Nikephoros, is more obscure. It is possible that these items refer to the artist and to the instruments that he employed, but it is more likely that they normally referred to the man who commissioned the work, and to the artist he employed to attain the final cause by executing the intention in his mind. Thus when Theodoros writes that he had illuminated his manuscript at the command of the Abbot Michael, Theodoros would be the organic cause, Michael the poetic; and the Emperor Basil I would be poetic cause of the building of the Nea. On this interpretation the Byzantine portrait of the donor is a portrait of the poetic efficient cause.

But it is the formal cause that is predominant. Nikephoros writes that the Form of Christ is the formal cause of an ikon of Christ. In the same fashion the Emperor's person would be the formal cause of an ikon of the Emperor. That implies that the formal cause determines the intrinsic importance of an image. The image of Christ is in itself more glorious than that of a saint, the image of an emperor more glorious than that of a prefect. This in turn effects the choice of the material cause.

The final cause now meant, I suggest, simply the purpose for which the image was made—the intention to make an image of a particular saint or emperor, or of the Virgin or of Christ, under a particular aspect. On this interpretation the intricate development of iconography in the Macedonian period was intended to make the final cause apparent. It is characteristically Byzantine that this is achieved by contrasting colours. Thus if Christ was shown in white it was for the Transfiguration, if in blue and gold it was for any other scene before His Crucifixion, if in purple and gold it was for the scenes following His Resurrection. Blue and variants of purple became the colours for the Mother of God; light green and blue for St Paul.[29] But the iconography was reinforced by the identification of a particular pose with a particular attribute—as in the conventions for the *panagia glykophilousa* representations of the Mother of God—and by the use of emblems and inscriptions sometimes in combination, as on the 10th-century images of Constantine and Justinian in Haghia Sophia.

But final and formal causality were closely associated; the details that made the final cause of a painting or of a mosaic obviously identifiable also made its formal cause immediately apparent. The primary object of a Byzantine artist of this period was to let the formal cause become translucent through the material.

10

The Macedonian Renaissance

THE PRESENCE OF SUCH ART THEORIES MUST HAVE
helped to determine the character of what has been termed
rather clumsily the Macedonian Renaissance. Three main
tendencies can be distinguished within the developments in
Constantinopolitan art between 842 and 1071: a fashion for the
reproduction of the antique; new rhythms in scene composition
perhaps influenced by court ceremonial and by the mimes; the
increasing presence of Islamic art motifs. Frequently all three
are combined in one object, as in the enamelled red glass bowl
in the treasury of San Marco.

Only the first tendency can be described as a renaissance, and
we have no evidence that it was a sudden rebirth. By far the
greater part of the art of the Iconoclast emperors has vanished,
since their palaces have disappeared and their systems of church
decoration were replaced by that of their Iconodule successors;
but it is possible that the art of the Macedonian emperors was in
direct development from theirs. There is much to suggest that
the three main tendencies that have been noted really evolved in
the lost court art of Theophilus (829–842).

Two 9th-century manuscripts[1] seem to show a direct descent
from the work of Iconoclast masters. The first consists of the
Homilies of St Gregory Nazianzen executed for the Emperor
Basil I; the second, a Psalter, is more difficult to date with any
certainty. Both were illuminated with magnificence. But the
illuminations in the *Homilies* that show the Cross alone still seem
characteristically Iconoclast. So too, perhaps, were the personified figures like the Night and the Dawn in the *Homilies* or
Melody in the Psalter since it was agreed throughout the controversies that personified figures were not ikons.[2] So too may

be the tendency to portray biblical figures as classical—so that
King David is shown as Orpheus in the Psalter. Possibly the
great mass of the reminiscences from Hellenistic illusionist
painting, in especial the use of the landscape, may have been
directly derived from Iconoclast wall-paintings. Often the
illuminations seem like wall-paintings transferred onto a page.

But though on this hypothesis many of the Hellenistic
elements in Macedonian painting were derived from those of the
Iconoclast court, there is evidence that at least until 1025 they
were being continually reinforced by direct reproductions of the
antique. Thus the St Matthew painted about the middle of the
10th century in the Stauronikita Codex 43 seems to be a direct
copy of a 2nd-century statue of Epicurus, and the two portraits
of St Luke[3] in the 10th-century British Museum Additional MS.
are derived from two variants of the Philosopher convention on
early-3rd-century sarcophagi.

For the antique would be equated with the classical and
would gain its prestige from the association with the literary
classics which were then so fashionable. Perhaps for the Macedonian patrons as for those of the Italian Renaissance the antique
appealed as also being the most modern. It seems likely that in
both periods the conception was used to cover any work of art
from before the mid-3rd-century transition and would tend to be
primarily associated with sculpture. Since technically an exact
reproduction of sculpture was never attempted the tendency
would be to render such reminiscences in painting.[4]

A desire for novelties was closely linked with the fashion for
the antique. Such novelties were found primarily in the naturalistic rendering of a deep emotion, conceived as ennobling, or in
the naturalistic portraiture of an individual, which would be at
once recognizable and idealized as in the mosaic of Leo VI in
Haghia Sophia. Again this may be linked with the cult of the

literary classics and especially with the fashion for Homer and for Euripides.

Yet even when Macedonian painting is most clearly classical in inspiration this is expressed in fresh rhythms. I am convinced that the paintings in the church at Castelseprio were 10th-century Byzantine, the work perhaps of two craftsmen who had been sent as part of an embassy from Constantinople to some Lombard prince. In the scene where the Angel tells St Joseph to take the Child and the Mother to the security of Egypt, the figure-work would be inconceivable without a Hellenistic background.[5] But in order to express the urgency of the warning the composition is like that of some far later ballet.

In the Paris Nazianzen the setting of the Visions, the personification of Night, the dawn-glow on the mountain-tops, even possibly the charnel of dead bones could be copies from a Hellenistic original and so could the central figure and its draperies; but not the stance of the figure, or the face or the gesture of the arms; those are the three factors that express the essential meaning of each picture.

There are new experiments in composition. At times it is strictly centralized, but frequently the centre of gravity is to the right of the picture space—like St Basil celebrating the Eucharist at Ochrida, Leo VI honouring Christ in Haghia Sophia, the Washing of the Feet in the catholicon of Hosios Loukas, and (to judge from reproduction) the seated Evangelist in the Koimesis at Nicea. The list could be multiplied. Perhaps it was the Byzantine custom to look at the picture from left to right and its message was thus made immediately apparent.

As the result of the Iconoclast controversy an image, and in particular the ikon that was also a scene, had come to be considered as a Word, a Logos. This helps to explain the essentially theological character so much Macedonian church decoration

assumed as soon as the Sacred Images returned. In a series of
five poems Ignatius the Magister describes the redecoration of
the church of the Virgin of the Fountain.[6] He writes on the
scenes placed there to represent the Annunciation, the Presentation, the Transfiguration, the Crucifixion and the Ascension.
When Michael the Amorian replaced the Sacred Images in the
Golden Hall of the palace a poet wrote: 'Thou dost picture the
Lord in colours, establishing by act the Logoi of the dogmas.'[7]

Yet what is unexplained is the actual rhythm of the figures,
which is so clearly intended to express the meaning of the scene
and which as already suggested possesses so many of the
qualities of ballet.

A possible source is the ceremonial of the Imperial court.
Again this was partly a legacy from the Iconoclast emperors, and
there is some evidence that it reached its full development in the
reign of Theophilus. It was an Imperial liturgy re-enacted un-
changingly by the Basileus and by his great officials, a series of
intricate scenes, from that considered appropriate for the
reception of foreign envoys to that of the Giving of the Robes
of Honour on the Thursday before Easter.

The 10th-century approach to this Imperial liturgy is suggested by the proem to the *Book of the Ceremonies* by Constantine
VII Porphyrogenitos: 'To neglect this ceremony and to sentence
it as it were to death is to be left with a view of an empire devoid
of ornament and deprived of beauty. If the body of a man was
not formed gracefully and if its members were casually arranged
and inharmoniously one would say that the result was chaos
and disorder. . . . To the end that we may not appear to disgrace
the majesty of empire by disorderly deportments we have
thought it necessary with laborious effort to gather from many
quarters all the ceremonies invented by the men of old. . . .
Culling as it were a bunch of flowers from the meadows we may

present it to the Imperial splendour as an incomparable ornament. . . . Hereby the Imperial power may be exercised with due
rhythm and order, the Empire may thus represent the harmony
and the motion of the Universe as it comes from its Creator.'[8]

Another source has been suggested—the Byzantine mime
and religious drama.[9] There is much evidence for the popularity
and prevalence of the secular mime, and very little for that of
acted religious drama. Still, direct influences from both might
well explain the new experiments in the expression of dramatic
tension which are sporadic in 12th-century Comnenian art. Some
influence from the secular mime may have been present in
mosaic as early as the age of Justinian, but in the Macedonian
painting it seems more likely that it was primarily exercised
indirectly as the ultimate source for some of the court ceremonial. The links between scenic representations from the New
Testament and the Apocrypha and written religious drama,
whether in dialogue or in hymnology, are obviously very close,
but it is not always easy to decide which has influenced the other.

Yet besides the influence on composition and on the representation of stance and gesture that was exercised by court
ceremonial and possibly by the mimes, the fashion for the reproduction of the antique was also affected by the contemporary
delight in geometrical experiment. This is sporadic in Macedonian painting and mosaic but can best be illustrated from a
single example: the painting of St Luke as an Evangelist in the
British Museum, in a 10th-century manuscript *de luxe*. Although
the seated figure is a reproduction from the antique, the use of
a wide gold background to emphasize its isolation may well be
an inheritance from Iconoclast art. The table at which St Luke
writes is in inverted perspective, widening as it recedes behind
him; the curve of his chair like that of the arch above him has
been designed to give an effect of inner space. A minutely

measured geometric scheme was first drawn on the vellum and the pigments laid on it. Even the drapery is treated geometrically for the linen is artificially crumpled and straight dark lines converge to indicate folds where none could have been naturally.[10] It is characteristic of the Macedonian period that the group of painters who illuminated the Paris Nazianzen composed masterpieces of Hellenistic figure-work as well as pages devoted to a single Cross.

The zest for mathematics and the desire to reproduce the antique were both due to a perennial Hellenism. In contrast there were contemporary Oriental influences sporadic in Macedonian art-forms.

It has been suggested as a possibility that some Byzantine painting may have been influenced by Chinese.[11] Historically this is not impossible. In the 9th and early 10th centuries the main trade west from China passed over land to Cherson on the Black Sea and so by sea to Constantinople. But it seems more likely that the similar conventions, especially in landscape painting, passed from West to East and that a Nestorian Christian art in Central Asia may have acted as their carrier.[12] More fundamental similarities may have been due only to fundamental resemblances between classical Chinese and Byzantine culture.

In contrast the influences from the Middle East are patent. The art and architecture of many of the Islamic courts had always been affected by that of Byzantium. But it would seem to have been only during the reign of Theophilus (829–842) that the influence grew reciprocal. Primarily this was probably the result of the new prestige that Islamic rulers had gained at Constantinople.

Two passages from the letters of Nicholas Mysticus illustrate this new attitude of respect. Nicholas was Patriarch of Constantinople from 901 to 907 and from 911 to 925. He stated:

'Two sovereignties, that of the Saracens and that of the Romans, surpass all sovereignty on earth like the two great lights of the firmament. For this one reason if for no other they ought to be partners and brethren.' He told the Emir of Khandak, the pirate ruler of Crete, 'Your wisdom cannot have failed to notice that the greatest among the high priests of God, the famous Photios, was united to the father of your highness by bonds of friendship. . . . Great in things divine and human he knew that even if the dividing wall of worship stood between us nevertheless the gifts of practical wisdom, sagacity, stability of behaviour, knowledge and all the other gifts that adorn and exalt human nature by their presence, kindle in those who love what is good a friendship for those who possess the qualities that they love.'[13]

Certainly from the early 9th until the early 12th century Islamic art seems to have possessed some of the prestige of fashion at Constantinople. It was perhaps conceived as novel and as bizarre and yet was closely enough allied to be intelligible. The relationship is illustrated by the use of Kufic script and its derivatives in Byzantine decoration and by the adoption of Islamic forms in ceramics, textiles and ivory-work. In the reign of Theophilus there had been close links with the Abbassid court at Baghdad. In the 10th century there was an oddly close relationship with the Ummayad khalifs at Cordoba; Byzantine mosaicists and sculptors decorated their palace at Medina az Zahra.[14] But after 969 it seems likely that the chief current of Islamic influence came to Constantinople by the direct trade route from the elaborate Fatimid court at Cairo. Direct Islamic influences on representation could only have occurred in purely decorative paintings of beasts or of trees or of feasting and hunting scenes. But the representation of purely Christian subjects could be affected indirectly by Islamic pattern and design copied from imported textiles or ceramics. Such indirect influences could at times be vital, for most of the new experiments in technique which diversify the developments of Byzantine painting consist of fresh combinations in pattern and colour.[15]

The close interrelation between Islamic and Byzantine art-forms is apparent in Amorian and Macedonian ceramics. Changes in pottery are always a useful index to changes in culture and from the late 8th century there is evidence for the development of new types. By the late 9th century a polychrome ware had been evolved which could be shaped either as vessels or as plaques. Pigments laid thickly on a fine white paste are covered by a translucent glaze; colours had deepened, perhaps as the result of the Iconoclast emphasis on the gold background, and deep green, deep red, deep brown and deep blue were in common use. There was a monochrome variant with identical technique. In another type a glaze that after firing was a green yellow was laid direct on a white body. Very gradually other types were introduced—forms of sgraffito ware with a white slip on a red body.

Yet in spite of much promise, later Byzantine ceramics never developed any equivalent to the great wares of the Persian area. Perhaps this was the result of the Byzantine emphasis on the material cause; clay could never have the prestige of ivory. Apart from the chafing-dishes, which were perhaps a necessity only to the rich, there seems something rather *bourgeois* about much Byzantine pottery. Its glaze is seldom of the quality to appeal to the sense of touch which was so highly prized among Byzantines. They held touch to be the most fundamental of the five senses and coterminous with life itself.[16] It seems likely that carved ivory and cloisonné enamel meant to the Macedonians what porcelain and jade meant to the court of the Sung emperors.

The art of the enamel could appeal to much that was charac-teristically Byzantine besides the tactile sense; to the appreciation of a precious material, and to the desire to create new colours and place them geometrically in novel juxtaposition. In contrast to so much Western champlevé-work with its thick bronze or copper backgrounds, Byzantine enamels normally had a golden background and the coloured enamels were framed in thin lines of pure gold. In the age of Justinian the enamel pigments were primarily light green turning to translucent emerald, and red turning to violet. By the 10th century these were being replaced by a more translucent violet and a brighter purple, by red blended with white, by turquoise and by sky blue; lapis lazuli was now being ground. It is significant for the Palaeologan future that there was no necessary connexion between enamel colours and natural colours; purple had long been the convention for the colour of hair, flesh tints were frequently pale green. This made it simpler for new colours to be placed experimentally against each other. As Professor Talbot Rice has suggested, the thin gold lines that divide the enamel fields took the place of the pencil lines of a drawing, and since they could be so easily bent there were always new possibilities in composition and design.[17]

The age of the Amorian and Macedonian emperors coincided with the climax in ivory-work as well as in enamels. But it is far harder to reconstruct the art standards by which carved ivory would be judged. Clearly the material was costly, since like silk before the late 6th century it was necessarily an import, but it has not yet been determined to what extent it was imported from India or from East Africa and the Sudan. It is not yet clear how far the ivories were gilded or painted, but it seems unlikely that they were pure monochrome. The execution was normally of such high quality that it is probable that they were always articles *de luxe*. Perhaps they were differentiated primarily by their function.

One group consists of rectangular jewel-boxes and bridal

18 THE CHARACTER OF THE MACEDONIAN RENAISSANCE
[*p. 122*]

19 THE ARCHANGEL MICHAEL
[*p. 130*]

caskets; with it could be linked carved elephant tusks to be used as hunting-horns or at the circus. Such caskets were already fashionable in the 9th century. One at least,[18] perhaps many more, can be associated with the Iconoclast emperors.[19] The motifs were drawn both from classical reminiscence and from contemporary Islamic art. There is a delight in the minute. There are clear relations to miniature painting and in some cases to the designs on textiles.

Quite a different kind of workshop seems presupposed by the religious and the official ivories. When caskets, these would be intended to be used as reliquaries; when panels, frequently in diptych or triptych form, they would be either holy ikons to be honoured, and possibly on occasion worn, or Imperial ikons to be distributed as gifts on the occasion of an enthronement or of an Imperial bridal. Amorian and Macedonian ivories are perhaps the last example of that division of Byzantine secular art from religious and official forms for which there is so much literary evidence in the time of Justinian. The two were to merge finally in the 12th-century Comnenian revival.

Many Macedonian art-forms seem to have reached their climax by the death of Basil II in 1025. The mosaic cycle at Hosios Loukas had been completed, his *Menologion* like his Psalter had marked the culmination of many tendencies in manuscript painting, the great Eagle Textile at Auxerre is probably from his Constantinople factory, the Zeuxippos. The mosaics in Chios at Nea Moni are commonly dated about 1040 or 1050, and there are such small masterpieces as the enamel dancing-girls in the crown of 'Constantine Monomachos'[20] (1042–1052). But it is perhaps significant that the Zoe panels in Haghia Sophia (1042–1057) although accomplished have none of the strength of the 10th-century mosaic of the Virgin flanked by the two emperors in the narthex.[21]

The *ekphraseis*, the description of a decorated church, had grown increasingly stereotyped. Scenes are described in an expected order, spectators are adjured to move their eyes swiftly, there is the conventional praise of gold and of multi-coloured marble, but there is no longer the zest of aesthetic appreciation that had marked the *Description* by Photios on the 9th-century church of the Nea.[22]

For Photios there are three elements in aesthetic perception, Joy, Wonder and an inner turmoil; here Photios is using the term that had been sanctioned by Scripture for the descent of the Angel into the Waters. These are caused simultaneously by sight and wrench the mind to ecstasy.[23]

There seems to be some parallel with music—a reference is made to the Thracian Orpheus striking upon his lyre.[24] Details of craftsmanship are highly praised, notably in the decoration of the pavement.[25] The recurrent emphasis is on the eyes. There is no sign of the antithesis between *nous* and *aisthesis* which is so marked in the 12th-century *Ekphrasis* by Nikolaos Mesarites.[26]

But by the middle of the 11th century the graphic arts were being eclipsed by rhetoric. Sight was no longer the queen of the senses, it had been replaced by hearing. Michael Psellos was born in 1018 and died about 1078. His writings emphasize a conception of the power of the word unparalleled since Nazianzen and Chrysostom. He notes in his *Chronographia*, 'It is testified of me that my tongue flowers with blossoms even in simple utterances and that without any effort of mine some natural fragrance is distilled from it. I should not have known this myself if many persons had not told me so during my lectures.' He stated in a letter to the Patriarch Cerularius, 'The Nile waters the ground for the Egyptians and my tongue does the like for their minds. Ask the Persians and the Ethiopians, they will tell you that they have admired me and sought me out, and now a man from the boundaries of Babylon has come to drink of my waters with an unquenchable thirst.' For Psellos as for his younger contemporary Theophylact 'art' means the art of rhetoric.

Had the Empire survived unbroken it seems likely that the graphic arts might have become sterile. They were however revitalized under the Comnenian emperors as part of the general Byzantine response to the challenge of a collapse. For during the later 11th century the Empire almost disintegrated, primarily through economic causes.

One such factor was a shift in world trade routes. Recent archaeological discoveries in the Indian Ocean area have shown that in the late 10th century the Fatimid khalifs in Egypt reopened the old sea route that led past South Arabia to the Far East; Cairo instead of Constantinople became the chief diffusion centre for Far Eastern goods. It was a misfortune for the Macedonians that this temporary fall in public revenue coincided with a period of financial maladjustment. The number of great landowners was increasing steadily since the prohibition of usury and the rise in agricultural prices had made land the most profitable investment for capital. There was also a development of great monastic estates normally exempt from taxation. Both these factors diminished the numbers of the free peasantry. After 1025 the strength of the great landowners threatened the immemorial power of the civil service, and the civil service and a free peasantry had been the basis of Macedonian greatness. It was a sign of the new political power of the landed magnates that they were relieved of the heaviest of their financial obligations during the weak administration of Romanos III (1028–1034). The extravagance of his successors exhausted the reserve in the Treasury and their financial expedients proved disastrous. The rights to farm taxes were sold either to firms of contractors or to individual landowners. Imperial estates were granted away for life in return for an immediate money payment. Successive debasements of the coinage reduced the value of the gold nomisma from twenty-four to twelve carats.

The power to resist had been weakened fatally. In 1065 Armenia was conquered by the Sultan Alp Arslan. In 1071 the Normans seized Bari, the last Byzantine outpost in the West. In the same year the Emperor Romanos IV was defeated and captured by the Seljuk Turks in a chance and unnecessary battle at Manzikert. Throughout the vital area of Asia Minor the balance of power swayed to the Seljuks.

11

Comnenians and Palaeologans

IT HAS BEEN CUSTOMARY TO CONSIDER THE LATIN SACK of Constantinople in 1204 as the end of an epoch. But in reality the epoch had ended with the loss of the greater part of Asia Minor after 1071. For it was the possession of Asia Minor which had made the East Roman Empire viable both militarily and economically and which had enabled it to survive the crises of the 5th and the 7th centuries.

What was left of the Byzantine State was saved from disintegration partly through the tenacity and astuteness of Alexios I Comnenos (1081–1118). But it only survived precariously among the sporadic avalanches of the Crusades and with a continuous strain upon its boundaries from the Seljuk Turks and from the Norman Kingdom of Sicily. Venice, once the successor to Ravenna as a cultural outpost of Byzantium, was now becoming a trade rival. The Comnenian emperors attempted to cope with these new dangers by an elaborate and too sophisticated diplomacy and by an increased use of mercenaries, but Byzantine diplomacy seemed chicanery to the new baronial societies of the West and the attempt at a military reconquest of Asia Minor failed disastrously when Manuel I was defeated at Myriokephalon in 1176. Yet Constantinople was still the City and the point of juncture where trade routes from east to west crossed those from south to north. The Jewish traveller Benjamin of Tudela records that Manuel I received twenty thousand gold ducats daily from customs dues and market dues. So much portable wealth was a temptation to Western adventurers and a stimulus to Venetian trade rivalry. As a result Crusaders stormed and sacked Constantinople in 1204. It is perhaps only surprising that this had not happened earlier.

Western rulers styling themselves emperors held Constantinople until 1261. Byzantine culture remained unbroken. Primarily this may have been due to the tenacity of Byzantine civil servants and scholars like Nikephoros Blemmydes and the Grand Logothete George Akropolites, who preserved a continuity in administration and in ceremonial at Nicea; here the court and the Patriarch had found refuge and here the Lascarid dynasty claimed to be the heirs of the Comnenians. Michael Palaeologos had been the 'urbane and courteous' guardian of the last Lascarid whom he blinded and replaced; when he recaptured Constantinople on the 25th of July 1261 the Imperial administration returned with him unaltered. So also, apparently, did Comnenian art-forms; at times it is oddly difficult to be sure which works were commissioned soon before the sack of 1204 or soon after the recapture of 1261.[1]

The mosaic cycle in the church of the monastery of the Chora provides a fairly fixed date for comparison.[2] It was commissioned by Theodore Metochites, who died in 1331 and who had been Grand Logothete to the Emperor Andronicus II Palaeologos (1282–1328). It seems likely that it was begun about 1310 and completed about 1320.

The links with the Deesis in the south gallery at Haghia Sophia and with the scenes from the life of Saint Euphemia may be explained if they also were Palaeologan. But the resemblances are even closer with a Bodleian New Testament[3] which is certainly 12th-century Comnenian and, although not so close, they are apparent in the illuminations in a Metaphrastes[4] which is probably about 1130 or 1140 in date. The Chora marks the final development of a style first apparent in the mosaic cycle from the life of the Virgin at Daphni and in the illuminations in the Paris manuscript of the *Homilies on the Virgin* by James of

Kokkinobaphos.[5] Both almost certainly belong to the reign of John II Comnenos who died in 1143.

Several factors would explain this continuity in Byzantine art during the Latin usurpation of the City. Artists as well as scholars may have found shelter and patronage at the court of Nicea. But it is also clear that a number of workshops continued to function at Constantinople under its Western rulers. Thus Mount Athos Iviron Codex 5, Paris B.N. Gr. 54, Princeton University Garrett M.S.2, Athens Nat. Lib. Codex 118 were all apparently illuminated by Greek artists for 13th-century Latin patrons and it seems most likely that this occurred at Constantinople. Besides, the wall-paintings at Boiana in Bulgaria about 1259 and at Sopocani (1258–64) are only really explicable if artists from Constantinople had been employed on them. Slav princes as well as the Angeloi in Epirus and the Comnenoi at Trebizond—the Byzantine rivals of the emperors at Nicea—could provide court patronage for the representatives of Comnenian court art. But perhaps the primary factor was the unbroken survival of Byzantine culture, scholarship and administration, preserved in microcosm at the Nicene court.

During the final phase of East Roman history from 1261 to 1459 the territories controlled by the Palaeologoi from Constantinople were so few that they only nominally formed an empire. Politically the East Roman State was obviously doomed. The army, now mainly mercenary, was negligible, the fleet only occasionally existed, the fortifications were becoming outmoded and would be rendered useless by the development of artillery. The civil service and the Imperial ceremonial went on unaltered. As late as 1395 the Patriarch Antonios wrote that though the Emperor Manuel II Palaeologos was surrounded by the Gentiles he was still the Lord and Governor of the Universe.

The eleven emperors who reigned in this period form a

relatively undistinguished series, although Michael VIII Palaeologos and John VI Cantacuzene were brilliant if conventional
diplomats and Constantine XI had a quality of greatness.[6] Some
had able ministers like Metochites but circumstances were
forcing them to rely on subtlety. The Empire was being exploited
economically both by Genoese and by Venetians and it was a
rhetorical convention to lament the vanished riches of the
Treasury and the poverty of the regalia; but it is beginning to
become clear that great wealth was still possessed and that the
standard of luxury was high. It was once held that poverty led
Palaeologan patrons to abandon mosaic for fresco, but this is now
untenable in view of recent discoveries: the mosaic cycle that has
been finally uncovered at the Chora; the mosaics discovered
in the church of the Pammakaristos; the 14th-century miniature
mosaics recorded at the Vatican, in the Hermitage Museum, at
Leningrad, at Chimay, at Berlin, in the Dumbarton Oaks
Collection, in the Victoria and Albert Museum and at Florence.[7]
A mark of the 14th-century court workshops was an apparent
delight in the use of precious materials—lapis lazuli and any
stones that could rank as jewels, or silver and gold. The great
mosaic of the Virgin and Child uncovered in the apse of Haghia
Sophia is almost certainly later than the earthquake of 1346.
The fashion for wall-paintings of fine quality is already apparent
in those of the 12th century at Nerez and in Cyprus and is foreshadowed in the 11th century at Ohrid. As a medium, painting
gave a wider scope for experiments in undulations and shades of
colour and in attempts to convey the plasticity of form.

The wealth in 14th-century Byzantium was due primarily to
a development in Central Asia. The Mongol conquests of the
13th century had created a 'Pax Mongolica' that stretched from
Pekin to Caffa in the Crimea. This had led to a great increase in
the Far Eastern trade that passed through Constantinople. A new

20 THE YOUNGER ALEXIOS COMNENOS

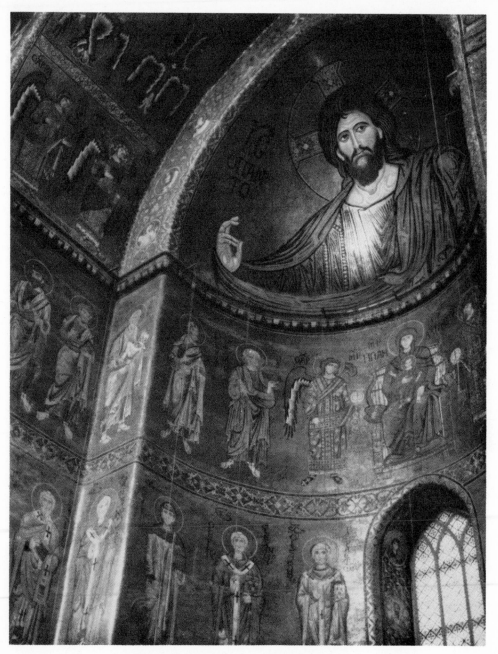

21 THE CHRIST OF MONREALE

trade route for Indian goods and in especial for pepper was also developing in the late 13th century. This led north to the head of the Persian Gulf, then overland to Trebizond and then by sea to Constantinople. By the early 15th century this had been expanded to the south-east by the establishment of Malacca as an Indonesian *entrepôt* and had become a main route for all the spice trade. At the same time there was an expansion into Europe. Westward and to the north Genoese merchants had now linked Constantinopolitan trade not only with Spain but with Bruges and Southampton. And at Bruges and London the Genoese met the northern traffic of the Hansa League. Another route passed from the Flanders cities down the Rhineland to Milan, then to Venice, then by sea to Ragusa and so overland to Constantinople.

All this world traffic brought prosperity not only to Constantinople but to its subordinate cities, Trebizond and Thessalonika and Mistra and Monemvasia. It may help to explain a new outburst of patronage of the arts. For the first time in Byzantine art history private patrons became common: Theodore Metochites, Alexis Apakaukas, Michael Tarchaniotes, Martha the wife of Michael Glabas, Maria Palaeologina, Euphrosyne Palaeologina, probably Michael Tarnikes, certainly Lascaris Khatzikis. It is true that all the men in this list were leading civil servants and that the women were members of the Imperial family grouping; it seems not unlikely that their wealth was due to perquisites.

But though there was wealth to the end of the Byzantine Empire it had become very unevenly distributed. The great riches of a few individuals suggest that the guild system was in decay and price controls relaxed. The factions at Thessalonika imply that the small traders and the artisans had combined against the officials and the rich. This new grouping of the economically oppressed would naturally be linked with the peasant serfs who had taken the place of the smallholders and who were burdened by the Imperial hearth tax as well as by forced labour.

Religious homogeneity, which had strengthened Byzantine civilization for five hundred years, was also vanishing. The religious schism between East and West had been very gradual. Relations had deteriorated sharply after 1054; they had been envenomed in 1204 by the brutal sack of the City and still more by the appointment of a Latin Patriarch. But from 1272 until 1453 there was a Party of Union pledged from whatever motive to re-establish full religious accord with the West. For the mass of the monks and of the people this Party of Union and such emperors as favoured it through diplomatic necessity were Latinizers and defilers of Orthodoxy. This cleavage grew wider through the Hesychast controversy.

Hesychasm as a school of mysticism was already recognizable in 11th-century Constantinople. In the 14th century it became fully articulate in the teaching of Gregory Palamas. Some practices in contemplation and the emphasis on the blinding vision of the eternal and uncreated Light of Godhead exposed it to attack from a group of theologians, some of whom were closely associated with the Party of Union. It was a misfortune that it became suspect at the court of the Palaeologan emperors through the political affiliations of some of its leaders with the faction of the Cantacuzenes. The monasteries on Athos became its stronghold. It became one more factor of disruption.

Yet perhaps it was precisely the existence of these tensions that made the last century of Byzantine culture also the most fertile. There were at least four Byzantine painters of genius between about 1330 and 1444: the Master of the Anastasis at the Chora, the Master of the Peribleptos at Mistra, the two Masters of the Pantanassa. The Thucydidean tradition in historiography which begins with Anna Comnena culminated in the 15th century with three major historians. Hellenistic love romances had been revived in 12th-century Byzantium with *Rhodanthe and Doricles, Drosilla and Charicles, Hysmenias and Hysmine*. These are obvious sources for the Old French *roman courtois* and therefore for all late Western novels. There are fresh if bizarre developments in the Palaeologan romances like *Rhodamne* and like *Chrysantza*. A tradition in satire that had begun with the 12th-century Prodromic poems grew coarser and more realistic. There is a sudden outburst of love lyrics. Gemistos Plethon, the most original of all Byzantine thinkers, died about 1450. Byzantine civilization was never more fertile than when it was destroyed.

The Harmony of Colours

IT IS BECOMING INCREASINGLY APPARENT THAT IN THE
history of Byzantine art the Comnenian and Palaeologan periods
should be considered as a single unit and that the movements once
thought characteristic of the early 14th century first developed in
the 12th; within one cultural framework art seems to develop in
an unbroken continuity. The Early Comnenian synthesis between
Macedonian court art and the narrative conventions derived from
a school of monastic painting is still formative in the 15th century.

This monastic school has been described as Cappadocian
from the wall-paintings found in that area of the Asia Minor
hinterland. These prove the existence of a tradition in religious
art quite distinct from that of the capital. The paintings at
Qaranleq, at Tokale Kilisse, at Qeledjlar Kilisse and at Tcharegli
illustrate the persistence of the style from the 9th until the 12th
century. It is at times crudely emotional; it has its own rhythms;
it is frequently marked by a vigorous brutal realism, by the
decision to emphasize the dramatic and by the successful intention to tell a clear story clearly.[1]

It is tenable that this style is only accidentally Cappadocian
and that the rock-cut chapels in that conservative province have
preserved the relics of a once widespread school of monastic
painting. Similar paintings probably dating from the 10th and
11th centuries have been discovered in the Latmos Caves near
Miletus. I have noted paintings of the same school in the crypt
church at Hosios Loukas and in Cyprus. There is a close relation
between the Cappadocian wall-paintings and a contemporary
group in Greek South Italy. It is possible that monastic journeymen painters carried the style from abbey to abbey and from one
cluster of hermitages to another.

There would be no aesthetic standards in such art for there would be no aesthetic purpose. It is improbable that they were intended to be either decorative or didactic; most likely they were placed there to be visual aids to meditation for a group of monks or for a single hermit. Often they possessed the raw vitality of a peasant art.

It was inevitable that this tradition should eventually blend with the city art of Constantinople and of Salonica. When a country monastery was given the rank of an Imperial foundation mosaicists from the Capital might still be sent to decorate the church as an Imperial Benefaction; as would seem to have happened at Hosios Loukas under Parnassus, at Daphni in Attica, and at Nea Moni on Chios. The personnel of town and country monasteries were at times interchangeable. There was a strongly Hellenist element in the 11th-century monastic revival and in foundations like Patmos which were devoted to learning.[2]

Perhaps the first evidence for the blending of this provincial 'Cappadocian' style with Constantinopolitan is from details of the mosaics at Nea Moni such as the gesticulating figure of Longinus. The wall-paintings in the medieval Cypriote churches show that the fusion could be a long process. There are two scenes in pure 'Cappadocian' style on the south wall of the first chamber of St Neophytos painted in 1194. The scene of the Scourging at the Pillar on the west end of the north wall of the church at Galata is a 'Cappadocian' derivative and this was painted as late as 1511. At Asinou and at Pedhoulas variants of the 'Cappadocian' tradition are combined with rather clumsy copies from Constantinopolitan pattern books. Yet by 1180 there was an artist working in Cyprus who painted in the new Constantinopolitan style. This was the Master of the Deposition at Haghios Chrysostomos; the dark body of Christ is stretched on the white shroud while His Mother presses her cheek to His. There is a close relation to the clearly Constantinopolitan paintings in the church of St Panteleimon at Nerez in Macedonia which are dated 1164. In both cases the artists with a supreme technical ability followed canons traditional in court art; the calculated contrast in the colours, a minutely measured rhythmic composition, the emphasis on the *eurhythmos* in the figures. In both there is a new emotional depth and range inconceivable in pre-Comnenian art and a new emphasis on the moment of dramatic tension.

Within a predetermined iconographic convention such tension could be best conveyed by experiments in contrasted colours and by the discovery of new rhythms in the grouping of the figures. In a 12th-century illumination[3] a headsman unsheathes his sword as the wind blows back his cloak and the martyr's red clad body sways abruptly towards a dark blue crag. When a Greek illuminated a manuscript[4] for a Latin patron he attempted to convey the tension of Christ's betrayal through the rhythms of a crowd of dancing figures.

Such experiments must have helped to develop another note common to much Comnenian illumination and some Comnenian ikons and to the 14th-century mosaic cycle at the Chora—the small scale of the figures as they move against a background at times as remote and as unlimited as the sky. Technically this may also be due to the pervasive influence of enamels. Often Comnenian art-forms seem to be Macedonian enamel-work translated into new media. This might explain not only the figure scale and the new combinations of 'unnatural' colours but the sporadic appearance, notably in ikons, of an art that had grown more flat, more patently geometric and more linear. If enamel-work grows rarer in this period it is perhaps partly because it is being replaced.

It may be suggested that the Comnenian synthesis is primarily from two elements. The forms are derived from variants of 10th-century Constantinopolitan art; the content has been affected by the monastic tradition with its realist emotionalism, its emphasis on dramatic tension, its attempts at continuous narrative. But there are other possible factors, new developments in 11th-century spirituality and a new social grouping among the patrons. Both perhaps rendered the traditional Constantinopolitan art-forms more receptive to the currents from 'Cappadocia'. The first would lead to a deeper appreciation of emotional tenderness and dramatic tension; the second might be responsible for the taste for narrative.

The characteristics in spirituality which Western medievalists associate with the Cistercian and Franciscan schools were already apparent in 11th- and 12th-century Byzantium. These were an essentially Christocentric devotion, an emphasis on each physical detail of the Incarnation, the spirit of the *Stabat Mater* and of the Crib. These were to be recurrent throughout Comnenian and Palaeologan painting. They find supreme expression in the 12th-century Constantinopolitan panel which is known as the Virgin of Vladimir. The representations of the Crib culminate in the 14th-century Nativity in the Peribleptos church at Mistra. There has been no greater representation of the Franciscan hymn of the *Stabat Mater* than the Still Virgin beneath the Cross in the late-14th-century Crucifixion scene from Thessalonika, now in the Byzantine Museum of Athens—or of that equally Franciscan hymn the *Dies Irae* than the 12th-century Christ in the dome at Daphni, or in the 12th-century Byzantine judgement scenes that face the altars at the cathedral of Torcello and at the church of Sant' Angelo in Formis. 'Franciscan' spirituality with all its emphasis on love and tenderness and its vivid eschatological afterthoughts had begun in the East a century before St Francis. Comnenian art may well have been one of its carriers westward.

The effects of a slight social shift among art patrons is of course more problematic. It is certain that from 1025 the families of the landed magnates in Asia Minor began to take a share in the Imperial administration. The great houses of the Comnenoi and the Dukai both belong to this grouping. At the beginning of the 12th century Anna Comnena in her *Alexiad*[5] places an emphasis on the significance of noble birth which is inconceivable in any earlier Byzantine writing and which is not repeated under the Palaeologoi. The civil service remained throughout a career open to talent and to the study of good letters. In the reign of Manuel I Comnenos (1143–80) Theodore Prodromos wrote of the results of learning, 'when he was studying he did not know the entrance to the Baths and now he takes the Baths three times a week. Once he had fleas as big as almonds and now gold pieces with Manuel's effigy upon them'.[6] The writings of George Akropolites[7] and of Thomas Magister[8] suggest how completely the rather civilian ideals of this section of the bureaucracy were to triumph at Nicea, but in the 12th century many of the Comnenoi showed a delight in personal prowess and in good horsemanship which was most probably derived from the baronial background to their house. How far was this social cleavage reflected in art patronage? The only evidence for the artistic tastes of the magnates on the Asiatic border is provided by the poem on Digenes Akritas.[9]

It was the hypothesis of Dr S. P. Kyriakides that the texts of *Digenes Akritas* represent two Dukas revisions of 1059–67 and of 1078–81 preserved in the versions in the Escorial and at Grottaferata and a Comnenian redaction of the first half of the 12th century.[10] This was only an hypothesis. But it may be taken as established that the poem was composed in the hinterland of Asia Minor sometime in the 11th century, that it was intended for recitation not in the market place or monastery but before some great lord, probably from its genealogical detail a relative of the house of Dukas.

22   THE CRUCIFIXION

23   THE RAISING OF LAZARUS
[*pp. 39, 140, 155*]

It seems clear that in this milieu the graphic arts were still highly prized. It is high panegyric of a heroine to write 'in truth the girl was like a picture painted' (line 1431): aesthetically, a quality of polished translucence was much valued; 'the floor of it he paved with onyx stones, so firmly polished those who saw might think water was there congealed in icy nature' (lines 3364 et seq.); and again 'shining marble throwing gleams of light' (line 3360). The hero Basil's flesh seems made of crystal. His bride is known by the glister of her beauty; 'the noble girl, her beauty ever gleaming brighter than peacock shone' (line 2490). The favoured colours would seem to be white, red and gold as in the description of the duel with the Amazon Maximo (lines 3012 et seq.). To these might be added green, as in the colouring of Basil's spear-haft (line 1231). The tint ascribed to white at this period is suggested by the line 'her face had copied the narcissus hue' (line 2493). The equation of white with the narcissus tint instead of with the 6th-century ivory tint or silver had already been suggested by the line in the 'Poem on the Spring' by John Geometres 'the narcissus gleaming whiter than the snow'. The red was probably a deep red, perhaps the 'stretched' red referred to in the *Description of the Church of the Holy Apostles* by Nikolaos Mesarites (xx, 5). In the *Akritas* the conventional comparison is with the rose (line 2572) and more oddly with the Imperial purple. The heroine's lips are tinted 'as with the chosen purple kings do prize' (line 1435). But it seems likely that at least by the 12th century the Imperial purple was normally a dark red; Mesarites notes in his *Ekphrasis* that the Imperial Chrysobulls were signed in the colour of the Blood of Christ. Gold would include not only the colour of gilt mosaic cubes but the favoured tint of crocus yellow. Blue could include violet but normally as in Mesarites (xx, 5) it was conceived as the same colour as the sky.

More significant than all this is the emphasis on narrative art.

When Basil built his palace on the Euphrates 'he laid out in the wings on either side reclining-rooms long, wondrous golden-roofed' where he could 'paint fair in gold mosaic' the triumphs of all who had 'shone in valour' (lines 3369 et seq.). These triumphs were shown in narrative form; 'he painted too the very moves of war' (line 3386). They were pictured stories drawn not only from the Old Testament and the Alexander legend but from the classics. 'The fabled wars, he painted, of Achilles, Agamemnon, the Fair. The Baleful Flight. Penelope the Wise. The Suitors Slain' (lines 3393 et seq.).

It is at least tenable that the taste for a continuous, dramatic, narrative sequence in pictorial art which survived under the Palaeologoi gained some of its first impetus from the tastes of this group of patrons. Perhaps they were also partly responsible for the sudden contemporary emergence of the Byzantine novel. In the 12th century Niketas Eugenianos describes the plot of his *Drosilla and Charicles* in his proemium; 'Flight. Wanderings. Waves. Captures. Violence of brigands. Imprisonment. Pirates', and at last the wedding-feast.

An *Ekphrasis* summarizes the aesthetic standards at Constantinople just before it was sacked by the Crusaders. This is the *Description of the Church of the Holy Apostles* by Nikolaos Mesarites[11] which is proved by intrinsic evidence to have been composed between 1198 and 1203. An antithesis is drawn between mind and sight, between *nous* and *aisthesis*. The Church 'does not please *aisthesis* more than it impresses the mind' (XIII, 2). 'The lines bring delight to *aisthesis*, they make their impress on the *nous*' (XIII, 8). Beauty is perceived by both, but it is perceived by sight as colour and by mind as a form of geometry. 'It fills the sight with beauty of colour and with the golden glimmer of its mosaics, it strikes the mind by its surpassing size, its skilled construction' (XIII, 2). Geometry is highly prized. 'Mathematics is the highest of the sciences' (XLII, 8). Reference is made to a mathematical proletariat who are concerned only with logistics and who teach simple reckoning: 'the calling by which they have lived and on which they grow old is commonplace and rude, wherefore they always look upon their pupils with a wild, an angry and a bitter eye' (X, 2 and 3). But a clear contrast is made between them and 'the people who are concerned with geometrical lines' (XLII, 7). 'Tones and harmony take their beginnings from arithmetic, the mediator and transmitter between them is geometry' (XLII, 8).

The same colours are singled out as in the *Akritas* poem; blue, red, white, gold. 'Sky blue, deep red and white' (XX, 5), 'golden glimmer' (XIII, 2). 'The robe of the God Man is coloured more with blue than with gold' (XIV, 8). But another is added, the 'iris-coloured light' of XIII, 9.

More significantly the mosaic scenes are described precisely as narratives and praised repeatedly for the dramatic quality of their details (e.g. XVII, XVIII, XXII). In this he was only reflecting 12th-century taste, but one theory suggests a trend in the future. Mesarites records the opinion that the five senses which are the organs of *aisthesis* belong to two different groups; sight and hearing in contrast to touch, taste and smell. 'Sight and hearing transmit to the brain the first contacts with the object of sensation', 'Touch, taste and smell refer sensations to the heart as soon as they encounter them' (XLII, 5). This would be to dethrone touch from the central position among the senses accorded to it by the Damascene and Nemesios. Emphasis has already been laid on the possible importance of the tactile sense in the Byzantine appreciation of textiles, enamels and ivories, wrought marble and *cosmati*-work. This would still be true of the 12th century, but apart from portable mosaics there was to be little to appeal to the tactile sense in Palaeologan art.

In a slightly obscure passage (XIV, 3) Mesarites praises an optical device in the representation of Christ in the dome. He appears to be leaning down from it as from a lattice and His head is the same size as the body as far as the navel.

Optical devices and experiments in perspective mark Byzantine art from the 12th to the 15th century. They seem to gain their impetus under the Comnenoi as an attempt to portray dramatic action within pictorial space.[12] Mosaics at Daphni will illustrate a transition in forms of composition,[13] for they fall into two groups, the first possibly dating from about 1100, the second probably a generation later. In the first, figures are grouped symmetrically on either side of a vertical axis that exactly halves the picture. The action is conceived as taking place within the real space of the church. No illusionism is needed for the scenes of the Annunciation and Baptism since real space is included in the curved surface of the mosaic; Gabriel gives his message to the Virgin across the physical space of a squinch. Some illusionism was used when the mosaic was on the flat surface of a wall; in the Crucifixion scene Christ's white body sways into the church from the black central vertical axis which is the upright of His Cross.

But in the other group by the Master of the Childhood of the Virgin the figures are placed in carefully calculated asymmetry not round a vertical axis but round another figure which is their centre of gravity, normally on the right side of the picture. There is a vertical axis but it is not central; normally it divides the picture space by a ratio of 1 to 2. At times there is an attempt to convey depth by the use of a high horizon line which again may divide the picture space horizontally by a ratio of 1 to 2 or of 2 units to 5. Thus in the Daphni mosaic of the Birth of the Virgin the centre of gravity is the body of St Anne in the right of the picture space; the six smaller figures are grouped round her; the picture space is divided vertically (ratio 1:2) by an axis that passes down through her right hand, it is divided horizontally (ratio 2:5) by the horizon line of her couch. Depth is conveyed since the Virgin is being washed in a basin in front of her mother's couch and therefore below the horizon line. Action is conceived as taking place within the pictorial space.

A similar technique was used about the middle of the century in the Byzantine mosaic of the Nativity in the Capella Palatina at Palermo. Here the centre of gravity is the figure of the Virgin in the right of the picture; twelve smaller figures are grouped round her. The composition is in the symmetrical convention; there are six figures on either side and a central vertical axis, dividing the mosaic, is marked by the ray from the Star of Bethlehem. But a horizontal line is provided by the rim of the manger and once again a Child is being washed in a basin below it and therefore in front of it. A further illusion of depth is given by the use of the Hellenistic rock motif as background and above all by the dark niche that frames the Virgin's body and forms the opening of the Cave.

Within a generation the use of recurring dark niches to give depth to an architectural background had become common; the scenes on the west wall of the transept at Monreale are an example; at times as in the Monreale Christ before Pilate, narrow doors open obliquely onto the picture surface at angles of forty-five and of seventy-five degrees. Pictured architecture and pictured thrones are shown curved. The optical devices that create the spatial depth in the Chora mosaics are being evolved through the 12th century to meet the needs of new styles of continuous narrative. But they presuppose an optical theory and a conception of *skenographia* that had been explicit since before Justinian, and these are composed from elements of Hellenistic illuminism that had been repeated in Macedonian manuscript illustrations: like the sloping ground in front of the jagged rocks on fol. 27 of the *Menologion* of Basil II.

It is tenable that these perspective devices grew too intricate in their application. Frequently there are two planes in a single picture, as in the 13th-century ikon of the Virgin in the Duveen Collection, where the flat plane of the gold background descends into the recessed plane of the curved throne. At times there seem to be two pictures in a single mosaic scene, as when the Virgin receives the purple at the Chora. But since according to Byzantine optical theory a picture was apprehended by being touched by rays from the eyes this was on occasion inevitable; when a narrative was depicted as occurring within pictorial space it was natural that its sequence should be followed detail by detail. The onlooker moved into a new imagined space within the ikon or within the wall. The *stil nuovo* of Giotto was at its most Byzantine in the use of a 'box-space' perspective to contain the dramatic tensions of its figure-work.

The zest for new experiments in perspective would seem to have lasted at least until the fall of the Empire. Lincoln College Greek MS. 35 is a 14th-century composite; additions were made to it in 1397, 1398 and 1402 (ff. 161–162^v). It contains a portrait group of the community at the convent of the Virgin of the Protovestiary at Constantinople which is in a different hand from its earlier illuminations and is possibly early 15th century. The artist had to convey the presence of twenty-nine figures grouped on a page of 21.4 by 15 cm. They recede in ascending tiers with the black of the monastic habit as their common foreground. The treatment is unique in Byzantine painting, yet it is a logical development from the technique used in the crowd scene in the early-14th-century wall-painting in the Afentiko church at Mistra.

The lower half of a painting, which has been dated approximately 1440, was discovered in the exonarthex of the Chora. A figure, probably from the dress some great official, stands before an enthroned Virgin and Child, perhaps offering Them a gift. Again this is technically unique in Byzantine painting. It may well have been stimulated by Italian *Quattrocento* influence. There is a 'natural perspective', and a humanist sense of the flesh beneath the textile covering. Yet it is still integrally Byzantine. The figures face each other in three-quarter profile as in a traditional Annunciation scene. The marble floor on which one stands and the Others are enthroned is the lower frame of the scene, part of a room that opens like a niche into the real space of the church. It is still not the 'window perspective' of the High Renaissance.

'Highlights' in painting become increasingly dominant from the 12th to the early 16th century. The experiments in their use may be taken as another form of experiment in optics. Either in dead-white or in bright colours they take the place of shade in later Western painting[14] and were clearly valued for their effect on modelling. Normally very carefully measured they could lead to such achievements in geometric painting as the Transfiguration scene in Paris[15] which can be dated between 1347 and 1355. But they had also perhaps a deeper function in an art in which composition was always conceived in terms of colour.

A late composite manuscript[16] contains a painting of St John the Evangelist which has been dated between about 1300 and 1340. It measures 25.5 by 19 cm. It contains eighteen different shades of colour. New tints would seem to have been achieved by mingling, by dilution and by the overlaying of one pigment upon another. They were applied with little relevance to the 'natural' colour of the objects depicted. The earliest known example of the new range of colours would seem to be the 13th-century wall-painting uncovered in 1959 in the church of Haghia

Sophia at Trebizond. Christ is shown in the Ascension scene in carefully graded tints of blue and orange.

The wall-paintings in the east chapel of St Sava outside Trebizond are dated by an inscription as 1411. The backgrounds are a bright black on a green. The colours used have been listed as white, red, red-brown, red-yellow, yellow-brown, gold-brown, bright grey, black-grey, blue-grey and grey-green, bright pink, bright blue, dark blue, blue-black, bright black, dark green and pale green.[17]

It seems likely that late medieval Trebizond possessed its own variants in Byzantine painting. It is becoming increasingly clear that it was a diffusion centre for art influences; north to Rumania and Russia, perhaps south to Irak and to the Persian area; diffusion centres are also receptive. It was ruled by its own dynasty who were subordinate to the emperors at Constantinople but autonomous. In contrast Mistra, the Byzantine headquarters in Greece, was inextricably linked with the life of the Capital. Since 1348 it had been the normal residence of the future successor to the Throne; it was also a normal place of exile for unsuccessful politicians. There is evidence for a frequent interchange in the personnel of the administration. In the quarter of the Monem-vasiotes, the 15th-century House of the Despot with its long halls and its elaborate arcading was in essence an annexe of the Palace at Constantinople. It seems licit therefore to deduce contemporary Constantinopolitan court taste from those Mistra paintings that date from between about 1350 and 1442.

A group of Byzantine churches still survives in the deserted 18th-century town of Mistra on the mountain-slope above modern Sparta. Scenes of a Nativity sequence were painted there in the monastery church of the Brontochion perhaps about 1350 or 1360. Only fragments of them remain; a bright green ox browses beneath the Crib, the ivory flesh tints of the priest Zachary are

24　THE NATIVITY
[*pp. 140, 155*]

25   THE VIRGIN BENEATH THE CROSS
[p. 145]

shaded in green and ochre; beyond, in the square domed chamber of the Imperial Charters, Angels with overlapping wings swerve among wine-red shadowing. A pathway from the Brontochion wavers down the mountain through small ruined houses to where the church of the Peribleptos, the Resplendent One, grows out of the hillside, half church, half cavern. There is no inscription by which the paintings there can be dated with certainty but it seems likely that they were completed shortly before 1400. The secular tradition in Byzantine art had now finally been absorbed in the religious.

There is a painting in the Peribleptos of a boy shepherd with a flute which is a Hellenistic pastoral, but the subject is an antiphon from the Christmas office: 'Silence thy flute O Shepherd and chant that tonight Christ is born, the Saviour, the Blessed.' In the Passion scenes in the nave, a dark bent Christ strains beneath the Cross or against a ladder among rough splashes of blue light. In contrast in the painting of the Divine Liturgy, Christ the Priest stands vested before the altar while towards Him and from Him come the lines of Angels bearing the bread and wine. For the subject is the antiphon 'Seeing the tribune of the altar stand trembling, O man cast down thy eyes, for within is the Christ daily sacrificed and all the ranks of the holy angels prostrate themselves before Him in fear and ritual.' The dominant is an orange shadowing upon white, and opal vestments fall from neck to ankle in still and living folds.

Above the Peribleptos on the walls of the church of the Pantanassa new colour combinations were achieved between 1428 and 1442: the Annunciation scene with the thin marble pillars and the quail beneath the wine-red pineapple of the fountain; the Raising of Lazarus with its stress on movement, the quick unwinding of the sere cloth, the dull ochre shadowing upon the marble, the small white flowers with chocolate leaves;

the Entry into Jerusalem, the high white donkey against a background of small vermilion houses crushed within a city wall of crocus yellow.[18]

The cause for the marked increase in the number of colours and for the fresh experiments in their combination is the main problem in any attempt to reconstruct Palaeologan aesthetics. East Roman art had become essentially polychrome, perhaps in the 5th century. It has been noted that novel colour combinations were praised by art critics of the period of Justinian and that under the Macedonians it was an axiom that shapes could only be perceived as colour. It has been suggested that colour experiments in Macedonian enamel-work influenced Comnenian manuscript illumination[19] and panel-painting.[20] Yet none of this adequately explains the increase of range in the palette of Palaeologan artists.

A clue to the developments in the final period of Byzantine art may be found in the philosophic preconceptions of its patrons. It was a link between the Comnenians and the Palaeologoi that in both periods a knowledge of philosophy was held to be a requisite of good administration. Perhaps it had come to take the place in the training of the civil servant formerly held by the study of good letters. In the late 11th century the encomium on Constantine Leichudes by Michael Psellos expressed the then immemorial ideal of the Byzantine Mandarin: 'He had moreover something harmonious and distinctive about him especially when he was proclaiming the Imperial Decrees as from on high.' But Psellos also notes that he always acted 'philosopher wise' and states in another encomium that 'there is nothing comparable to philosophy'.

This was one of the traditions that were maintained at the court of Nicea. In his *Oration on John Dukas Vatatzes* in 1254 George Akropolites writes 'it was not from riding or archery that he first set out on his way . . . it was from the study of philosophy itself, . . . it was from the highest knowledge of the Nature of Being'. 'States will have rest from their evils and be compassed about by blessing when rulers become philosophers, philosophers rulers'.[21] Nikephoros Blemmydes wrote to Theodore Lascaris: 'Kingship that is not philosophic is far from God.'[22]

Under the Palaeologoi, Thomas Magister wrote that philosophy 'is the guide and companion on the path of duty' since it enables man to distinguish 'the things that exist forever and have no coming and going from the things that come and go but never truly exist'.[23] Throughout the writings of Theodore Metochites and Gemistos Plethon, philosophy and administration are assumed to be inextricably interwoven.

From the 11th to the 15th century Byzantine philosophy was not only far more esteemed and more vital than under the Macedonian emperors,[24] it was predominantly Neo-Platonist. It has already been noted that John the Damascene, Theodore the Studite, and Nikephoros of Constantinople had discussed the causality of paintings and the nature of aesthetic perception in Aristotelian terms. The last Byzantine philosopher to be dominantly Aristotelian was Michael of Ephesus, who composed his commentaries on the *Politics* and the *Ethics* between 1070 and 1080. The antithesis between Platonism and Aristotelianism must never be overstressed in any discussion of medieval thought.[25] There is evidence for a close study of the Aristotelian *Animalia* under the late Comnenoi.[26] At least as a name Aristotle was revered by Metochites. Outside the court circle, there are signs of an Aristotelian revival shortly before the Turks took the City.

But to use a phrase from the late-12th-century eulogy on Eusta-thios of Thessalonika, even when Byzantine thinkers were Peri-patetics they had become peripatetic in the groves of the Academy and along the Porch. From the mid 11th to the mid 15th century, from Psellos to Plethon, Byzantine philo-sophical speculation was dominated by the group defined by Anna Comnena as 'Proclus and Plato and the two philosophers Porphyry and Iamblichus.'[27]

During its last phase the Byzantine world view became ex-plicitly very close to that of the late 3rd century. There was even some revived knowledge of Plotinus; a passage on the culmina-tion of philosophy in the funeral oration delivered by Michael Psellos is modelled on *Ennead* I, 6.[28] Under Alexios I Comnenos (1081–1118) two other factors had helped to re-establish finally the Neo-Platonic view of world order. The court theologian Euthymios Zigabenos was integrally influenced by St Gregory of Nyssa, the most Middle Platonist of all Greek Fathers. Anna Comnena records the court fashion for the reading of the commentaries by St Maximus on Pseudo-Dionysius;[29] the mystical theory of both Maximus and Pseudo-Dionysius is Neo-Platonist.

Byzantine philosophy remained synthetic. The memory of Pythagoras was venerated, partly perhaps because of the prestige of mathematics; in the 14th century the conversation of the daughter of Theodore Metochites was praised as resembling that of Pythagoras. In the 15th century Neo-Pythagorean texts are among the sources used by Gemistos Plethon. Some knowledge of Stoicism had also survived, perhaps through manuals. This is illustrated not only by the many references to the Porch and by Plethon's praise of suicide but by the recurrent emphasis on the world as a single living organism.

But from the 11th to the 15th century the synthesis is primarily Platonist. Byzantine church painting was to become increasingly a form of liturgy, a ritual through which an initiate could move securely in a shadow world intent upon the world it shadowed. Novel colour combinations would never be considered as violating Nature. For Nature was conceived as a unit, as an intelligible order following intrinsic laws, as primarily incorporeal not corporeal. Michael Psellos had written 'when you have stolen from intelligence the incorporeal quality in things and have realized the light within the body of the sun then you will turn with keenest vision to the incorporeal itself'.[30] Re-enacting the forms of Nature, art re-enacted their reality, not necessarily those surface phenomena which were fading into unreality precisely as they materialized.

So again in portraiture. A series of official portraits begins with the 12th-century mosaic of the Empress Irene uncovered in Haghia Sophia; it includes the Theodore Metochites of the Chora, the Court Ascetic at the Brontochion and the young Palaeologan prince at Megaspilaeon; it culminates in the painting of the 15th-century minister Manuel Lascaris Khatzikis on the walls of the Pantanassa. These portraits are official yet utterly individual, for as in the 3rd century the artist is attempting to express through material detail the unique *pneuma* of each subject, his 'Spirit and his Breath.'

Parallels with abstract art became increasingly recurrent in Byzantine painting though more often in sections of a composition than in the composition as a whole.[31] Perhaps these were attempts to convey the dynamism of Reality through patterns moulded in inevitable colours. Byzantine painting like Byzantine mosaic may have been apprehended as a form of music in which colour combinations were the harmonies.[32]

At least this could explain the Palaeologan creation of so many distinct tints. For the first essential in harmony was conceived as multiple diversity. About 1328 Theodore Metochites wrote of Harmony in his *Hypomnematismoi* 'there cannot be harmony among musical instruments, nor can they blend in a symphony and concordance of tune, if all the notes of the strings are identical, with an equal pitch, a unison of sound and a similarity of time'. There cannot be a 'rhythmical and musical order' unless there is 'distinction between different parts'.[33] The second essential was unity. Metochites adds that in a Harmony 'parts different in kind are composed, ordered and concentrated into a unity' and it is 'as a form of unity that it is viewed and defined'.

Perhaps for the Palaeologan painter the more multiple the diversity of tints the deeper the colour unity that they could form. It would be a re-enactment of the central problem of medieval Byzantine philosophy, the relation of the multiple to the One.

Byzantine civilization had always been a corporate whole centred not so much on the person as on the mind of the Emperor conceived as a ray of the Divine Wisdom. It therefore could not survive the killing of the last Emperor and the taking of the City by the Turks in 1453. Neither Mistra nor Trebizond were given time to develop into a new Nicea. The Imperial administration was shattered for ever.

But the vitality of the Palaeologan Empire is shown by the long survival of its influence after its destruction. For a hundred and eighty years Greek Christian painting is a Byzantine afterglow. The Osmanli Sultanate, the successor State upon the Golden Horn, preserved great fragments of ceremonial and organization and much private custom—the Audiences, the Sublime Porte, the Baths—and transmitted much of them as far east as the court of the Grand Mughal at Agra. The late-15th-century court of Moscow was to be polarized towards the memory of East Roman autocracy. In the West Byzantine influences were less recognized but more pervasive. In the last decades of the Empire, as the civil service dwindled, an increasing number of scholars were forced to live precariously by their learning. Many left the Capital—at first for Mistra or for Corcyra, later for Italy—in search of patrons. They included men of original talent like Bessarion at Rome, of high scholarship like Lascaris at Venice, of enterprise like Argyropoulos at Paris, as well as many members of an academic proletariat suddenly dependent on their wits alone. The characteristic Renaissance quality which is misdescribed as Machiavellian may have owed much to these *Graeculi* with their essentially civilian ideals, their traditional veneration for statecraft and their delight in astute subtlety. Wherever the Italian Late Renaissance spreads there seem to be echoes, however faint, from 15th-century Constantinople; in the conception of the Prince, or of the Minister, or of the Diplomat, and in the beginnings of a lay bureaucracy. Though Byzantine civilization was first forgotten and then travestied in the West, something of Byzantium remained wherever there was a belief in the dominance of cold Mind.

The Succession in the Imperial Sovereignty

A chronology of the East Roman emperors may be of some use for purposes of cross-reference. The names of the Augustae have been added when they participated publicly in the power of their sons or husbands or preserved the continuity of one of those loose-knit family groupings that formed the Byzantine equivalent to the West European dynasty. An attempt has been made to maintain the same system of spelling as throughout the volume. A number of East Roman names have their recognized English equivalents which it would be pedantic to ignore; Constantine or John or Basil. Many have gained, rather arbitrarily, recognized English abbreviations, like Marcian, Justin and Justinian, or forms of transliteration like Heraclius. But apart from these cases there does not seem to be adequate justification for Latinizing and for replacing 'k' by 'c', 'os' by 'us', 'oi' by 'i'.

379–395	Theodosius I
395–408	Arcadius
408–450	Theodosius II
450–453	Marcian and the Augusta Pulcheria
453–457	Marcian
457–474	Leo I
474	Leo II
474–491	Zeno and the Augusta Ariadne
491–515	Anastasius I and the Augusta Ariadne
515–518	Anastasius I
518–527	Justin I
527–548	Justinian I and the Augusta Theodora
548–565	Justinian I
565–578	Justin II
	(and the Augusta Sophia)
578–582	Tiberius II
582–602	Maurice
	(and the Augusta Constantina)
602–610	Phokas
610–641	Heraclius
641	Constantine III and Heracleonas
641–668	Constans II

668–685	Constantine IV Pogonatos
685–695	Justinian II Rhinotmetos
695–698	Leontius
698–705	Tiberius III
705–711	Justinian II Rhinotmetos
711–713	Philippikus Bardanes
713–716	Anastasius II
716–717	Theodosius III
717–741	Leo III The Isaurian
741–775	Constantine V Kopronymos
775–780	Leo IV
	(the Augusta Irene)
780–797	Constantine VI
	(the Augusta Irene)
797–802	The Augusta Irene
802–811	Nikephoros I
811	Staurakios
811–813	Michael I Rhangabe
	(the Augusta Procopia)
813–820	Leo V
820–829	Michael II The Amorian
829–842	Theophilus
842–867	Michael III
867–886	Basil I The Macedonian
886–912	Leo VI
912–913	Alexander II
913–959	Constantine VII Porphyrogenitos
	(the Augusta Helena)
959–963	Romanos II
	(the Augusta Theophano)
963–969	Nikephoros II Phokas
	(the Augusta Theophano)
969–976	John I Tsimisces
	(the Augusta Theodora)
976–1025	Basil II
1025–1028	Constantine VIII
1028–1034	Romanos III Argyros
	(the Augusta Zoe)
1034–1041	Michael IV
	(the Augusta Zoe)
1041–1042	Michael V Kalaphates

1042	Zoe and Theodora
1042–1055	Constantine IX Monomachos
1055–1056	Theodora
1056–1057	Michael VI Stratiatikos
1057–1059	Isaac I Comnenos
1059–1067	Constantine X Dukas
1067–1071	Romanos IV Diogenes
	(the Augusta Eudokia Macrembolitessa)
1071–1078	Michael VII Dukas
1078–1081	Nikephoros III Botaniates
1081–1118	Alexios I Comnenos
1118–1143	John II Comnenos
1143–1180	Manuel I Comnenos
1180–1183	Alexios II Comnenos
1183–1185	Andronicus I Comnenos
1185–1195	Isaac II Angelos
1195–1203	Alexios III Angelos
1203–1204	Isaac II Angelos and Alexios IV Angelos
1204	Alexios V Dukas
1204–1222	Theodore I Lascaris
1222–1254	John III Dukas Vatatzes
1254–1258	Theodore II
1258–1259	John IV
1259–1282	Michael VIII Palaeologos
1282–1295	Andronicus II Palaeologos
1295–1320	Andronicus II and Michael IX
1320–1328	Andronicus II
1328–1341	Andronicus III Palaeologos
1341	John V Palaeologos
1341–1354	John VI Cantacuzenos
1376–1379	Andronicus IV Palaeologos
1379–1390	John V Palaeologos
1390	John VII Palaeologos
1391–1425	Manuel II Palaeologos
1425–1448	John VIII Palaeologos
1449–1453	Constantine XI Palaeologos

Notes

For easy reference I have put the pages to which the notes belong in the headlines. The following abbreviations have been used:

B.M. Add. MS.	British Museum Additional Manuscript
B.N.	Bibliothèque Nationale
Byz. Zeitschr.	*Byzantinischer Zeitschrift*
De Imag.	*De Imaginibus*
Hist.	*Historia*
Hom.	*Homilies*
In Mt.	*In Matthaeum*
J.H.S.	*Journal of Hellenic Studies*
J.R.S.	*Journal of Roman Studies*
Paed.	*Paedagogos*
Pat. Graec.	*Patrologia Graeca*
Rév. de l'art chrét.	*Révue de l'art chrétienne*
Röm. Mitt.	*Römische Mittelalters*
Sac. Concil.	*Sacrorum Conciliorum nova et amplissima collectio*

I

Byzantine Aesthetics

[1] Cf. Agathias, *Hist.*, Lib. v, 6, c.

[2] This can only be finally established when the new X-ray processes have been applied to the blue wash design which probably survives upon the intermediate layer of plaster beneath most Byzantine wall-paintings.

[3] *Alexiad*, III, 3.

[4] *Hom.* I, 4 (Migne, *Pat. Graec.*, XLVIII, col. 705).

2

The Third-Century Transition

[1] Unless otherwise cited the evidence as to medallions and coins utilized in this chapter may be found published in H. Mattingley and E. A. Sydenham, *The Roman Imperial Coinage* (1933). It may be noted how deeply I am indebted to A. Alföldi for this interpretation of Gallienus.

[2] The last known use of the type of Gallienic philosopher-sage is on a panel of Saints Cosmas and Damian now in the National Gallery, London. It is signed by Manuel Tzanes and has been dated between 1660 and 1675.

[3] *De Vita Plotini*, §§4, 12.

[4] *Ennead* VI, 7, 22.

[5] *Ennead* I, 6, 1.

[6] *Ennead* v, 8, 1.

[7] *Ennead* I, 6, 3.

[8] *Ennead* v, 8, 1.

[9] *Ennead* I, 6, 2.

[10] A. Grabar, *Byzantine Painting* (Skira, 1953), p. 39. Cf. A. Grabar, *Plotin et les origines de l'esthétique médiévale* (Paris, 1945).

[11] *Ennead* I, 6, 1.

[12] Loc. cit.

[13] Ibid., 6, 3.

[14] *Ennead* VI, 7, 21.

[15] For the place of Proclus in the traditions that stemmed from that of Porphyry and Plotinus and for his influence at Byzantium cf. E. R. Dodds, *Proclus. The Elements of Theology* (Oxford, 1933).

[16] Cf. Gervase Mathew, 'The Christian Background', *Cambridge Medieval History*, IV, Chapter 2.

[17] *The Banquet of the Twelve Virgins*, Logos 11, section 2.

[18] Cf. Gervase Mathew, 'The character of the Gallienic Renaissance,' *Journal of Roman Studies* (1943), in which some of these ideas are further developed.

3

The Mathematical Setting *p. 23-*

[1] St Gregory of Nyssa, *Catechetical Oration*, VI, 2.

[2] These phrases are from St Gregory Nazianzen, *Orations*, 45, section 7.

[3] The history of Byzantine mathematics has not yet been studied fully. It seems probable that the period of creative geometry ended with the age of Justinian. But in the 9th century Leo the Mathematician was greatly valued for his innovations, though these seem to have been primarily in mechanics. The decimal system was first used in a 12th-century *scholion* on Euclid. A Byzantine treatise on Indian methods of calculation was composed in 1252. About 1290 Maximus Planudes describes his own method of extracting a square root 'which I claim as a discovery made by me with the help of God'. In the 14th century there is much evidence for fresh activity in applied mathematics both in the circle of the Grand Logothete Theodore Metochites, and in that of the Master of Requests, George Khatzykes.

[4] I follow the classification in Proclus's *In Euclid. I* but it should be noted how much of it was derived through Geminus from Aristotle (*Physics*, 11, 2; and *Posterior Analytics*, 1, 13).

[5] For this interpretation of Nicomachus I am indebted to Sir Thomas Heath's *Greek Mathematics* (Oxford, 1921), I, pp. 97–112.

[6] Ed. Pistelli (Teubner, 1894).

[7] Ed. Hoche (I, Leipzig, 1864; II, Berlin, 1867).

[8] *The Banquet*, Logos 8, section 11.

[9] Loc. cit. It is worth comparing the exposition of Mystic Number in St Gregory Nazianzen, *Orations*, 41, 2-4.

[10] I have taken this use of *belopoeika* from the treatise of that name by Heron of Alexandria, ed. Wescher, 1867. In the classification by Proclus the craft is termed *organopoike*.

[11-12] Ed. W. Schmidt (Teubner, 1899).

[13] Ed. V. Prou (1877).

[14] Sir Thomas Heath notes 'Hultsch's considered criterion is as follows: "The Heron texts which have come down to our time are authentic in so far as they bear their author's name and have kept the original design and form of Heron's works, but are unauthentic in so far as being constantly in use for practical purposes they were repeatedly re-edited and in the course of re-editing were re-written with a view to the particular needs of the time." ' Heath, *Greek Mathematics* (Oxford, 1921), II, p. 308.

[15] Ed. F. Hultsch (1876-8).

[16] Proclus, *In Euclid. I*, 8-12.

[17] O. Demus, *Byzantine Mosaic Decoration* (1948), p. 13.

[18] Ed. J. L. Heiberg-H. Menge (Teubner, 1895).

[19] Cf. MS. Laurentian 28, 3, and the 12th-century MS. Vind. Gr. 31, 13.

[20] O. Wulff in *Byz. Zeitschr.*, XXX (1930).

[21] Ed. Heiberg-Menge (Teubner, 1916).

[22] *Heronis Opera*, II, ed. W. Schmidt.

[23] G. Huxley, *Anthemius of Tralles* (1959).

[24] P. A. Michelis, *An Aesthetic Approach to Byzantine Art* (Batsford, 1955), p. 139.

[25] For these references I am indebted to Dr E. Panofsky.

[26] Cf. A. Grabar, *Plotin et les origines de l'esthétique mediévale* (Paris, 1945).

[27] Cf. the photograph in *American Journal of Archaeology* (1942).

[28] Edge-figures in such mosaics are also broadened by being placed in a wider posture than the others as in the scenes of 'The doubting of St Thomas' and 'Christ washing the feet of His disciples' in the catholicon of Hosios Loukas.

[29] E.g. the Apostles in a main cupola.

[30] E.g. the scenes from the lives of St Peter and St Paul in the cathedral of Monreale.

[31] Robert Byron first drew my attention to this passage in the poem on Haghia Sophia by Paul the Silentiary, though it will be noted that I have slightly altered his translation in *The Byzantine Achievement* (1929). Cf. lines 198 to 220 in Part II of the *Description of Haghia Sophia*.

[32] Ed. G. Friedlein (Teubner), p. 21.

4

p. 38-   *The Hidden Meaning*

[1] For the ambiguities of some Byzantine symbols cf. E. Kitzinger, 'Studies in late antique and early Byzantine Floor Mosaics', *Dumbarton Oaks Papers*, VI (1951).

[2] A close study of the Old Testament Trinity attributed to Andrei Rublev has led me to conclude that it is most probably Constantinopolitan of about the year 1400. This would explain the obvious relationship with Sienese *Trecento* painting—so inexplicable in early-15th-century Moscow.

[3] Cf. M. Rostovtzeff, *Dura-Europos and its Art* (1938), pp. 130 et seq.

[4] *The Banquet*, Logos 6, section 3, ed. G. N. Bonwetsch (Leipzig, 1917). There is an admirable English translation: *St Methodius. The Symposium*, by H. Musurillo (1958).

[5] Cf. Jocelyn Toynbee and John Ward Perkins, *The Shrine of St Peter and the Vatican Excavations* (1956), pp. 72 et seq.

[6] *The Banquet*, Logos 9, section 1.

[7] Cf. G. Rodenwaldt, *Jahrb. des Deutschen Arch. Institut*, LI (1936).

[8] Reproduced in F. Cumont, *Mystères de Mithra* (ed. 1913), fig. 21.

[9] Cf. F. Wirth, *Römische Wandmalerei* (1934), pp. 165 et seq.

[10] Sometimes referred to as Baebia or Hermophile. Cf. F. Gerke, *Vorkonstanische Sarkophage* (1940), pp. 120 et seq.

[11] For a full (but not definitive) discussion cf. F. Dolger, *Ichthys* (1927).

[12] Cf. Clement of Alexandria, *Paed.*, III, 59; Origen, *In Mt.*, XIII, 10; Tertullian, *De Baptismo*, 1; Ambrose, *In Hex.*, LV, 6; and the inscriptions of Aberkios, Alexander, Vibia, Pektorios.

[13] E.g. a lamp from a Christian cemetery at Carthage now in the British Museum. Cf. R. P. Delattre, *Rév. de l'art chrét.* (1892), pp. 133–4.

[14] Cf. K. Weitzmann, *Greek Mythology in Byzantine Art* (1951).

5

The Phase of Integration *p. 48–*

[1] *Panegyric*, VII, 21.

[2] E.g. *Theodosian Code*, XI, 7, 3.

[3] Cf., e.g. the *Maritus* of 12 March 312; the *Nemini* of 14 June 321; the *Quae Adulterium* of 3 February 326.

[4] Cf. *Theodosian Code*, V, 17, 1; IX, 12, 1; II, 19, 1.

[5] Cf. *Theodosian Code*, V, 9, 1; IX, 3, 1; VIII, 5, 2; IX, 18, 1.

[6] *Opera*, ed. Hertlein (Teubner, 1875), 453 b.

[7] Cf. P. J. Alexander, *The Patriarch Nicephorus of Constantinople* (Oxford, 1958), pp. 27–8.

[8] *Opera*, ed. Hertlein, 255 a.

[9] Ibid., 202 a.

[10] Ibid., 68 c.

[11] Ibid., 289.

[12] Ibid., 88.

[13] *Theodosian Code*, XVI, 1, 2.

[14] E.g. *Theodosian Code*, VI, 5, 2.

[15] E.g. *Theodosian Code*, VI, 1, 3; III, 12, 3 (396). Cf. C. N. Cochrane, *Christianity and Classical Culture* (1940), p. 326.

[16] Christian Lucas, 'The Curatores Rei Publicae of Roman Africa', *J.R.S.* (1940), xxx, Part I, p. 72.
[17] Cicero, *De Oratore*, III, 15, 57.
[18] *Opera*, ed. Hertlein, 422.
[19] *Theodosian Code*, XIV, 1, 1 (357).
[20] John Lydus, *De Magistratibus*, ed. R. Wuensch, III, cap. 26.
[21] Ibid., 28.
[22] *Theodosian Code*, I, 6, 9 (385).
[23] *Theodosian Code*, VI, 5, 2 (384).
[24] Ibid., 13, 1 (413).
[25] Ibid., 24, 4 (387); VI, 23, 1 (415).
[26] A. Alföldi, *Röm. Mitt.* (1934), XLIX, pp. 1 et seq.
[27] A review in *The Times Literary Supplement*, 21 October 1960.

6

p. 62– # The Age of Justinian

[1] Gervase Mathew, 'Byzantium', *Concise Encyclopaedia of World History* (1958), p. 177.
[2] Agnellus, 'In edificiis et in mechanicis operibus,' *Liber Pontificalis*, XXIV, 8, ed. A. Testi Rasponi (1924), p. 167.
[3] E.g. St John at Ephesus (probably 535–46).
[4] E.g. St Irene at Constantinople (532).
[5] E.g. Sts Sergius and Bacchus at Constantinople (526–37) and San Vitale (547).
[6] E.g. Sant' Apollinare in Classe by Ravenna (534–49).
[7] *Ennead* VI, 7, 22. Cf. Gervase Mathew, 'The Character of the Gallienic Renaissance,' *J.R.S.* (1943), p. 69.
[8] *Planudean Appendix*, epigram 225.
[9] Ibid., epigram 244.
[10] A. M. Andreades, 'The Public Finances', *Byzantium*, ed. N. Baynes and H. Moss (1948), pp. 71 et seq.
[11] Gervase Mathew, 'Byzantium', *Concise Encyclopaedia of World History* (1958), p. 177.
[12] The most recent study on Anthemius is that by G. L. Huxley, *Anthemius of Tralles* (1959).
[13] Agathias, *Hist.*, Lib. V, 6.
[14] Procopius, *Buildings*, I, 1, 24.
[15] For the details in this account, Agathias, *Hist.*, Lib. V, 6–7. Cf. the panegyric on Anthemius by Paulus Silentiarius in his *Description of Haghia Sophia*, ed. B. G. Nieburh, lines 267–78.
[16] From the Fragmentum Bobiense printed in G. L. Huxley, *Anthemius of Tralles* (1959), p. 21.
[17] Ibid., p. 25.

[18] Ibid., p. 25.

[19] 'On the Paradoxes of Mechanics', *Mathematici Graeci Minores*, ed. J. L. Heiberg (1927). The translation here used is that of G. L. Huxley in his *Anthemius of Tralles* (1959), pp. 6 et seq.

[20] John Lydus, *De Magistratibus*, ed. R. Wuensch, III, cap. 30.

[21] Ibid., cap. 14.

[22] 'And if ever he did visit a church as if to pray and keep vigil he did not behave in the least like a Christian, but putting on a rough cloak proper for a priest of the old faith which people are now accustomed to call Hellenic he would repeat all through the night certain unholy words which he had previously rehearsed.' Procopius, *Wars*, I, 25, 10.

[23] Procopius, *Wars*, V, 3, 5 et seq.

[24] Procopius, *Buildings*, I, 1, 61–2.

[25] Presumably this would only apply among the educated. The anecdotes in the *Pratum Spirituale* of John Moschos illustrate the strength of popular Christianity in the 6th-century East Roman Empire among one section of the common people and in the lower middle class. Cf. N. H. Baynes, *Byzantine Studies* (1955), pp. 261–70.

[26] Rufinus the Domestic, *Palatine Anthology*, Book 5, epigram 12.

[27] Julianus the Prefect, ibid., Book 7, epigram 32.

[28] Macedonius the Consul, ibid., Book 7, epigram 566.

[29] *Planudean Appendix*, epigrams 335–62 (printed in the Loeb edition of the *Anthology*, vol. 5, pp. 361 et seq.).

[30] Ibid., epigram 357.

[31] Ibid., epigram 342.

[32] Ibid., epigram 352 (cf. epigram 381).

[33] Ibid., epigram 344.

[34] *Palatine Anthology*, Book 9, epigram 809.

[35] This is the description, the *Ekphrasis*, by Christodoros printed in the Loeb edition of the *Anthology*, vol. I, pp. 59–91.

[36] *Planudean Appendix*, epigram 381.

[37] Ibid., epigram 384.

[38] Ibid., epigram 382.

[39] Ibid., epigram 80.

[40] Paulus Silentiarius, ibid., epigram 278 (cf. epigram 277).

[41] Leontios, ibid., epigram 283.

[42] Leontios, ibid., epigram 284.

[43] Paulus Silentiarius, ibid., epigram 277.

[44] Ibid., epigrams 284, 286, 287. All are by Leontios the Scholastic and the ikon was publicly displayed in the Sosthenion (epigram 284).

[45] Agathias, *Palatine Anthology*, Book 7, epigram 602.

[46] Leontios, *Planudean Appendix*, epigram 272.

[47] Cyrus, *Palatine Anthology*, Book 9, epigram 808.

[48] Paulus Silentiarius, ibid., epigram 653.

[49] Nilus, *Planudean Appendix*, epigram 247.

[50] Julian the Prefect, *Palatine Anthology*, Book 9, epigram 738. For Julian the

Prefect's conception of art note his phrase 'the flame that gives life is *Techne*' in epigram 87 of the *Planudean Appendix*. Cf. Paulus Silentiarius, ibid., epigram 57.

[51] *Palatine Anthology*, Book 1, epigram 10.

[52] Leontios, *Planudean Appendix*, epigram 245.

7

p. 78–   # The Official Programme

[1] E.g. the silver dishes from Constantinople (527–63) now in the Hermitage at Leningrad that represent Aphrodite in the tent of Anchises and a goatherd with his dog, or the Silenus silver fragment of the same period and provenance, now in the Dumbarton Oaks Collection, or the statue of Herakles and the Hydra now in the museum at Ravenna. Or the fishing boy on the silver casserole, the nereid on the silver vase, and the Atalanta and Meleager on the silver dish, all in the Hermitage, all Constantinopolitan and all securely dated 610–29. With this last group there should be placed the Herakles on the silver bucket at Vienna. For a stylistic analysis cf. John Beckwith, *The Art of Constantinople* (1961), pp. 40 et seq.

[2] The dating of the floor mosaics discovered at the Great Palace is still undecided. It was first suggested that they belonged to the period of Theodosius II (408–50). But there seems to be some archaeological evidence that the floor was laid after a reconstruction under Marcian (450–7) and recently two later dates have been proposed, 578–82 and 567–78. Cf. *The Great Palace of the Byzantine Emperors* (First Report 1947); (Second Report 1958, pp. 161 et seq.); John Beckwith, *The Art of Constantinople* (1961), pp. 29 et seq. I am inclined to hold that they belong either to the period of Anastasius or to that of early Justinian.

[3] Agathias, *Palatine Anthology*, Book 1, epigram 34. Cf. Nilus the Scholastic on an ikon of the Archangel, ibid., epigram 33.

[4] *Palatine Anthology*, Book 1, epigram 59.

[5] Ibid., epigram 67.

[6] Ibid., epigram 76.

[7] Ibid., epigram 75.

[8] *Planudean Appendix*, epigram 62.

[9] Ibid., epigram 63.

[10] Ibid., epigram 64.

[11] Agathias, ibid., epigram 41.

[12] Leontios, ibid., epigram 32.

[13] Leontios, ibid., epigram 37.

[14] Cf. R. Delbrueck, *Consulardyptychen* (1929), nn. 9 et seq.

[15] Cf. K. Weitzmann, *Illustrations in Roll and Codex* (1947).

[16] As Emmy Wellesz has noted, 'They are all written in the same Greek script, its metal shining against the purple vellum of the page. It is possible to point out in the Genesis illustrations a number of features which can be paralleled in the other two codices, we find certain figures in all three manuscripts which are as similar in

type as they are in the expressiveness of their faces and in their characteristic gestures and they wear the same costumes: some animals, some buildings and other objects appearing in the different codices have great resemblance to one another.' E. Wellesz, *The Vienna Genesis* (1960), p. 14.

[17] Paulus Silentiarius, *Description of Haghia Sophia*, Part II, lines 340 et seq.

[18] I should record that I have long been doubtful of the early date commonly ascribed to the Charioteer Silk in the Cluny and have suspected that it belongs to the period of Iconoclast emperors in the late 8th century. I note that I am supported in this view by Mr John Beckwith in his *The Art of Constantinople* (1961), p. 58.

[19] Cf. Procopius, *Buildings*, I, I, 60—purple, crimson, white, green.

[20] E.g. 'As with the chosen purple Kings do prize.' *Digenes Akritas*, line 1435.

[21] Cf. the statement of Rufinus the Scholastic: 'Your feet are whiter than those of silver Thetis.' *Palatine Anthology*, v, 48.

[22] Paulus Silentiarius, *Description of Haghia Sophia*, Part III, lines 50 et seq.

[23] Ibid., lines 90 et seq.

[24] It seems tenable that in the 6th century silver as a metal was more admired than gold. Thus Procopius notes that the inner sanctuary of Haghia Sophia was made beautiful by forty thousand pounds weight of silver. *Buildings*, I, I, 65.

[25] Paulus Silentiarius, *Description of Haghia Sophia*, Part III, lines 120 et seq.

[26] Cf. the description of the colour scheme in the palace of the Chalce: 'The white is set off with waving lines of blue.' Procopius, *Buildings*, I, x, 20.

[27] Paulus Silentiarius, *Description of Haghia Sophia*, Part III, lines 130 et seq.

[28] Cf. 'Some rival the emerald some simulate the flames of fire.' Procopius, *Buildings*, I, x, 20.

[29] E.g. 'Glittering and elaborate beauty'. *Palatine Anthology*, Book I, epigram 10.

[30] E.g. 'The whole building is overlaid with pure gold which adds glory to beauty the light reflected from the marbles shine out in rivalry with gold.' Procopius, *Buildings*, I, I, 54. Cf. the description of the martyrion of Anthimos in *Buildings*, I, VI, 13.

[31] *Palatine Anthology*, Book I, epigram 10.

[32] Procopius, *Buildings*, I, I, 60.

[33] These are now in Room 6 of the museum at Ravenna. They are fragments of small circular panes from seventeen to twenty-six centimetres in diameter. Besides purple-blue there are some of red-purple and of gold and green tints.

[34] Cf. 'One might imagine that one had come across a meadow with flowers in full bloom.' Procopius on Haghia Sophia, *Buildings*, I, I, 60.

[35] Paulus Silentiarius, *Description of Haghia Sophia*, Part II, lines 190 et seq.

[36] Ibid., lines 273 et seq.

[37] Ibid., line 285.

[38] R. G. Collingwood, *Roman Britain* (1932), p. 116.

[39] Of course this would also apply to the fourth form of adornment of the interior of buildings which is not described by Paulus Silentiarius—the representations in mosaic of the Imperial Victories. Procopius, *Buildings*, I, 10, 15–16.

[40] *Theodosian Code*, XIII, 3, 4.

[41] Theodore of Studios, *Epistulae*, 2, 46 (Migne, *Pat. Graec.*, XCIX, col. 1249 C–D).

[42] O. Demus, *Byzantine Mosaic Decoration* (1948), p. 12.

[43] *Palatine Anthology*, Book 1, epigram 10.

[44] Procopius, *Buildings*, I, 1, 28.

8

p. 94– ## The Evolution of the Image

[1] E.g. Justin, *Apology*, I, 9, 1. *Athenagoras, Supplicatio*, CC16–18.

[2] The first Christian expression of this conception would seem to be in Basil of Caesarea, *De Spirito Sancto*, C.18, a text much quoted among later Iconodule theologians.

[3] This citation was derived from P. J. Alexander, *The Patriarch Nicephorus of Constantinople* (1958), p. 27.

[4] Julian, the *Letter to Theodoros*, Loeb edition by W. C. Wright, II, 309.

[5] Also preserved in the *Praeparatio Evangelica*, Book III.

[6] Cf. N. H. Baynes, *Byzantine Studies* (1955), pp. 226 et seq., 'The icons before iconoclasm', in especial the citations, pp. 231–5.

[7] For the whole problem of the relationship between relics and ikons cf. A. Grabar, *Martyrium* (2 vols., Paris, 1943, 1946); in especial vol. 2, chap. 8.

[8] The classic account of the origin of such an ikon is in the sixteenth chapter of the third book of *De Fide Orthodoxa* by St John of Damascus, the Damascene: '... and when the painter could not paint because of the light that shone from His countenance the Lord Himself put a garment over His own divine and life-giving face and impressed on it an image.'

[9] E.g. images in the church of St Demetrios at Salonika.

[10] The text is in Mansi, *Sac. Concil.*, XI, 977 e.

[11] Cf. *Analecta Bollandiana*, 67. *Mélanges Paul Peeters* (1949), pp. 165 et seq.

[12] Canon 15 of the Iconoclast Council of 754 anathematizes any who shall not confess 'the Mother of God to be higher than every creature whether visible or invisible and does not with sincere faith seek her intercession'. Canon 17 anathematizes any who deny the profit of the invocation of Saints.

[13] P. J. Alexander, *The Patriarch Nicephorus of Constantinople*, p. 141. The reference given there is to the Cozza-Luzi edition of the *Epistulae* that I have not used—No. 41, p. 34.

[14] *The Seven Ecumenical Councils* (Vol. 14, of the Nicene and post-Nicene Fathers), p. 550; Mansi, *Sac. Concil.*, XIII, 377 d et seq.

[15] O. Demus, *Byzantine Mosaic Decoration* (1948), p. 6.

[16] E.g. St John of Damascus, the Damascene, *De Imaginibus*, III, 16 (Migne, *Pat. Graec.*, XCIV); Nikephoros, *Antirrhetikos*, I, 2–8 (Migne, *Pat. Graec.*, C).

[17] *De Fide Orthodoxa*, IV, cap. 15. Cf. *De Imaginibus* I, 4.

[18] *De Imaginibus*, III, 6.

[19] *De Fide Orthodoxa*, IV, cap. 16.

[20] The primary meaning of *proskynesis* in 787 would seem to be a salutation as a sign of reverence. 'When offering salutations to the life-giving Cross we sing

together "we give *proskynesis* to thy cross O Lord and we also give *proskynesis* to the spear which opened the life-giving side of thy goodness"; this is clearly a salutation and is so called, and its character is evinced by our touching the things mentioned with our lips: "to God alone do we render Latreia".' Letter from the Synod to the Augusti, Acts of the Second Council of Nicea (printed in *The Seven Ecumenical Councils*, p. 573).

[21] These arguments are developed in *De Imaginibus*, III, 27 et seq.

[22] *De Imaginibus*, I, 21.

[23] Ibid., 17.

[24] Ibid., 18.

[25] Ibid., 19.

[26] Acts of the Second Council of Nicea, Session I, printed in *The Seven Ecumenica Councils*, p. 535.

[27] Cf. the poem describing the effect on the Golden Hall of the Great Palace when Michael III restored the Sacred Images there. *Palatine Anthology*, Book I, epigram 107.

[28] E.g. the Virgin of the Blachernae and the Virgin of the Chalkoprateia within Constantinople and the Virgin of the Pege outside the Golden Gate.

[29] Cf. Migne, *Pat. Graec.*, CLV, col. 338 et seq.

[30] Ibid., col. 305 et seq.

[31] Cf. Gabriel Millet, *Récherches sur l'iconographie de l'Evangile* (1916), pp. 25 et seq.

[32] E.g. B.M. Egerton MS. 1139 F, 7b; or Judas at the Last Supper in the mosaic on the west wall of the south transept at Monreale.

[33] E.g. the Angel in the Annunciation scene at Daphni; the Virgin in the Nativity scene at Daphni; Christ in the Anastasis at Nea Moni; the Virgin in the Nativity and Christ in the Baptism at Hosios Loukas. Yet it should be stressed that this is not necessarily for purpose of prayer. At Nea Moni Adam and Eve are shown in three-quarter profile as they are being rescued by Christ. In the narthex at Haghia Sophia Leo VI is shown three-quarter profile as he worships the Divine Wisdom. In B.N. MS. gr. 510 Ezekiel is three-quarter profile when he receives the Divine Illumination. Presumably those who made contact with such images attempted in some fashion to join themselves with them.

9
Amorians and Macedonians

[1] Gervase Mathew, 'Byzantium', *Concise Encyclopaedia of World History* (Rainbird MacLean: Hutchinson, 1958), pp. 178–9.

[2] *Corpus Scriptorum Historiae Byzantinae*, XI, 337 et seq.

[3] Cf. the chapter on 'Public Finances' by A. Andreades in *Byzantium*, ed. N. H. Baynes (1948), pp. 71–86.

[4] St Athanasius, St Basil of Caesarea, St Gregory Nazianzen, St Gregory of Nyssa, St John Chrysostom, St Cyril of Alexandria. In the mid 9th century St John of Damascus was added to their numbers. It seems likely that the writings of the Pseudo-Dionysius were always on the fringe of the Canon.

[5] Compiled by Constantine Cephalas probably between 911 and 959.

[6] *Antapodosis*, VI, c, 5.

[7] On the other hand it should be noted that Constantine VII was praised for this mastery of the craft of painting. But the encomium continues: 'But who could enumerate how many artisans the Purple Born corrected? He corrected the stonemasons, the carpenters, the goldsmiths, the silversmiths and the blacksmiths and in all the Emperor appeared as the best.' Cf. John Beckwith, *The Art of Constantinople* (1961), p. 68.

[8] The *Book of the Eparch*, cap. 22, sections 1–3, ed. J. Nicole (Geneva, 1893).

[9] Note also the two signatures on the Elephant Silk at Aachen (probably 980–1000), and the names of Simeon and of Staurochios on the 11th-century doors at Amalfi and St Paul Outside the Walls.

[10] *Poetics*, 1448b, 15 et seq.

[11] *Athenaeus*, XII, 543 c.

[12] *Republic*, X, 597.

[13] J. W. Mackail, *Select Epigrams from the Greek Anthology* (1906), p. 54.

[14] *Palatine Anthology*, Book 1, epigram 33.

[15] Ibid., epigram 34.

[16] *Planudean Appendix*, epigram 244.

[17] *De Anima*, III, 3, 6.

[18] Ibid., 3, 14.

[19] Migne, *Pat. Graec.*, XCIX, col. 1220b et seq.

[20] Ed. Auvray, 1891, p. 111.

[21] *De Fide Orthodoxa*, II, cap. 17.

[22] Ibid., cap. 18.

[23] Ibid.

[24] Text published in P. J. Alexander, *The Patriarch Nicephorus* (1958), p. 211.

[25] Migne, *Pat. Graec.*, C, col. 748d.

[26] *De Fide Orthodoxa*, II, cap. 18.

[27] *Antirrhetikos*, II, 13 (Migne, *Pat. Graec.*, C, col. 357b.).

[28] Published in P. J. Alexander, *The Patriarch Nicephorus*, p. 204. Cf. *Antirrhetikos*, III, 35 (Migne, *Pat. Graec.*, C, col. 432b.).

[29] O. Demus, *Byzantine Mosaic Decoration* (1948), p. 90.

10

p. 122– # The Macedonian Renaissance

[1] B.N. Gr. 510 and B.N. Gr. 139.

[2] *Antirrhetikos*, II, 15.

[3] B.M. Add. MS. 28815, fol. 76 v and fol. 162 v.

[4] Gervase Mathew, *Byzantine Painting* (1950), p. 4.

[5] K. Weitzmann, *The Fresco Cycle of Santa Maria di Castelseprio* (Princeton, 1951).

[6] *Palatine Anthology*, Book 1, epigrams 109–13.

[7] *Palatine Anthology*, Book 1, epigram 107.

[8] *De Ceremoniis*, 1, 1–2, ed. A. Vogt.

[9] Cf. Madame Cottas, *Le Théatre à Byzance* (Paris, 1931).

[10] Cf. Athens, Nat. Lib. Cod. MS. 56, fol. 4 v. The tendency is first apparent in B.N. Gr. 510. The St Luke is B.M. Add. MS. 28815, fol. 76 v.

[11] Cf. David Talbot Rice, *Byzantine Art* (1954), p. 150.

[12] Still it remains possible that small articles *de luxe* may have been imported from China; the stylized birds on the ivory casket at Troyes suggest some such model.

[13] Translated in *Social and Political Thought in Byzantium* (1957), p. 116. (Text in Migne, *Pat. Graec.*, III).

[14] Cf. H. Terrasse, *L'Art Hispano-Mauresque* (1932), pp. 116–25.

[15] Gervase Mathew, *Byzantine Painting* (1950), p. 5.

[16] St John of Damascus, *De Fide Orthodoxa*, II, cap. 18; Nemesios of Emesa, *De Opificio Hominis*, cap. 9.

[17] David Talbot Rice, *Byzantine Art* (1954), p. 189.

[18] Cf. K. Weitzmann, *Greek Mythology in Byzantine Art* (1951).

[19] A. Grabar, *L'Empereur dans l'Art Byzantin* (1936), p. 169.

[20] This is clearly not the crown of Constantine Monomachos since it is a female diadem (cf. the crown of the Empress Irene in the mosaic at Haghia Sophia). The plaques suggest that it is either a crown of the Empress Zoe or of her fellow-Augusta Theodora. Zoe seems the more probable.

[21] Other evidence for a decline in aesthetic standards in Constantinople is provided by the Monomachos diadem studied as a whole and by the serpentine medallion inscribed with the name of Nikephoros Botaniates now in the Victoria and Albert Museum. Cf. John Beckwith, *The Art of Constantinople* (1961), pp. 107 and 118.

[22] *Hom.* III (Migne, *Pat. Graec.*, CII, col. 563 et seq.).

[23] Ibid., 569 a.

[24] Ibid., 567 d.

[25] Ibid., 569 c. Much more work is needed on the Macedonian pavement decoration. It seems likely that there were fresh developments in *Opus Alexandrinum* and that hollows were made in the marble and filled with contrasting colour. *Cosmati*-work may prove to be the most characteristic Macedonian legacy to medieval Western art.

[26] Nikolaos Mesarites, *Description of the Church of the Holy Apostles*, XIII, 2 and XIII, 8, ed. Glanville Downey, *Transactions of the American Philosophical Society* (1957).

II

Comnenians and Palaeologans   *p. 135–*

[1] Thus when I was working on the Deesis mosaic uncovered in the south gallery of Haghia Sophia I was inclined to place it as middle-12th-century Comnenian, and so finally was Professor Whittemore. Mr John Beckwith has recently suggested

that it is late-13th-century Palaeologan (*The Art of Constantinople* (1961), p. 134). Working on the wall-paintings in the buried church of St Euphemia in Constantinople I was inclined to place them perhaps about 1170. Mr Beckwith has recently proposed an early-14th-century date (op. cit., p. 145). It is significant that both systems of dating are tenable.

[2] For the discoveries in the church of the Chora (also referred to as the Karije Camii or the Kahrieh Djami) cf. the reports by Dr Paul Underwood in the *Dumbarton Oaks Papers* from 1955 to 1960; vols. IX and X (pp. 253 et seq.), XI, pp. 172 et seq.; XII, pp. 235 et seq., and 267 et seq., XIII, pp. 187 et seq.; XIV, pp. 223 et seq.

[3] Bodleian MS. Auc. T. Infra I. 10 (Misc. 136).

[4] B.M. Add. MS. 11870.

[5] Paris, B.N. Gr. 1208.

[6] Gervase Mathew, 'Byzantium', *Encyclopaedia of World History*, p. 134.

[7] Cf. John Beckwith, *The Art of Constantinople* (1961), p. 137.

12

p. 142– ## The Harmony of Colours

[1] Cf. R. P. de Jerphanion, *Les Eglises Rupestres de la Cappadoce*, four volumes of texts, three of plates (Paris, 1913 to 1941).

[2] For the character of the monastic setting cf. J. M. Hussey's classic *Church and Learning in the Byzantine Empire* (1937), and her *Ascetics and Humanists in Eleventh-Century Byzantium* (1960).

[3] B.M. Add. MS. 11870, fol. 104.

[4] B.M. Egerton MS. 1139, fol. 7b.

[5] *Alexiad*, III, 2; VII, 7; IX, 6; X, 5; XII, 2. Cf. G. Buckler, *Anna Comnena* (1929), p. 52.

[6] Theodore Prodromos to John Comnenos, ed. D. C. Hesseling and H. Pernot, p. 72.

[7] Cf. *Oration on John Dukas Vatatzes*, cap. 20, ed. A. Heisenberg, II, 27.

[8] Cf. 'On the Praise of Wisdom and Culture', cap. 25, ed. Mai, III, 168. It should be noted that while Akropolites composed his *Oration* at Nicea in 1254 Thomas Magister survived to be an official of Andronicus II who succeeded in 1282. Cf. Ernest Barker, *Social and Political Thought in Byzantium* (1957), pp. 159–73.

[9] *Digenes Akritas*, edited and translated by John Mavrogordato (Oxford, 1956). The citations in the chapter are from this edition and with the exception of the last, are from Professor Mavrogordato's translation.

[10] S. P. Kyriakides, *O Digenes Akritas* (Athens, 1926).

[11] Nikolaos Mesarites, *Description of the Church of the Holy Apostles*, ed. Glanville Downey, *Transactions of the American Philosophical Society* (1957).

[12] Cf. O. Demus, *Byzantine Mosaic Decoration* (1948), pp. 77–8.

[13] Cf. P. A. Michelis, *An Aesthetic Approach to Byzantine Art* (1955), pp. 156 et seq.

[14] Cf. David Talbot Rice, *Byzantine Art* (1954), p. 150.

[15] B.N. Gr. 1242.

[16] B.M. Add. MS. 5112, fol. 134.

[17] It should be stated that in this case I have no first-hand knowledge of the object discussed; the painting has been uncovered by Mr David Winfield while working for the Russell Trust.

[18] Gervase Mathew, *Byzantine Painting* (1950), pp. 5 and 22. I owe my interest in the colour combinations at Mistra to Robert Byron.

[19] E.g. B.N. MS. Gr. 1208 (the sermons of James of Kokkinobaphos).

[20] E.g. a small group of Comnenian panels in the monastery of St Katherine on Mount Sinai on which I worked in 1961. Dr Weitzmann has noted a tendency towards 'an increasingly dematerialized style' in 11th- and 12th-century art: *Greek Mythology in Byzantine Art* (Princeton, 1951), p. 207. It might be suggested tentatively that this too is partly the result of the influence of enamels.

[21] George Akropolites, *Oration on John Dukas Vatatzes*, cap. 20, ed. A. Heisenberg, II, 27.

[22] Nikephoros Blemmydes, *On Kingship*, cap. 1, ed. A. Mai, II, p. 609.

[23] Thomas Magister, *The Second Oration*, cap. 7, ed. A. Mai, III, p. 179.

[24] Michael Psellos asserts 'Philosophy when I first studied it was moribund as far as its professors were concerned and I alone revived it untutored by any master worthy of mention.' *Chronographia*, ed. E. Renauld (1926), p. 186; trans. E. Sewter (1953), p. 127; cf. J. M. Hussey, *Ascetics and Humanists in Eleventh-Century Byzantium*, p. 6. For the character of classical learning under the Macedonians, cf. the article by A. Dain in *Dumbarton Oaks Papers* (1954), N. 8, pp. 44 et seq.

[25] The fact that at least four Aristotelian texts were translated into Latin at the Norman court at Palermo between 1143 and 1180 suggest that they still possessed the prestige of fashion at Constantinople.

[26] E.g. the glosses in Late Comnenian minuscule on the text of the *Animalia* in Corpus Christi College MS. 108.

[27] *Alexiad*, v, 9.

[28] Ed. Sathas, v, 445.

[29] *Alexiad*, v, 9.

[30] Cited by J. M. Hussey, *Church and Learning in the Byzantine Empire* (1937), p. 74.

[31] The easiest hypothesis to explain Byzantine systems of composition is that the optical rays from the eyes were held to move along the surface from left to right.

[32] It is perhaps relevant that two qualities seem especially prized in Byzantine colour combinations; the colours are in contrast and the colours blend. Thus in the 11th century John Mauropous writes of an object 'its song is clear and melodious', 'two contrasting colours are wonderfully blended together', epigram 100, ed. de Lagarde, p. 51.

[33] Theodore Metochites, *Hypomnematismoi*, ed. C. G. Muller and T. Kiesling, p. 633.

Bibliography

In so far as possible the footnotes in this study have been limited to primary sources since it was intended to be the result of individual research; with three exceptions I have worked personally on every object that has been mentioned in it, even incidentally. Yet it might be of value to list contributions to the study of Byzantine art which have been published since the last war and which have been found particularly illuminating. It should be emphasized that this list is in no way exclusive.

BECKWITH, John, *The Art of Constantinople* (London, 1961).
    The Veroli Casket (London, 1962).
BERTELLI, Carlo, *La Madonna di Santa Maria in Trastevere* (Rome, 1961).
BUCHTHAL, H. (and KURZ, O.), *A handlist of illuminated oriental Christian Manuscripts* (Warburg Studies, vol. 12, London, 1942).
DEMUS, Otto, *Byzantine Mosaic Decoration* (London, 1948).
    The Mosaics of Norman Sicily (London, 1950).
    'Two Palaeologue Icons in the Dumbarton Oaks Collection'. *Dumbarton Oaks Papers*, XIV (1960).
    The Church of San Marco in Venice (Dumbarton Oaks Studies, 1960).
DODD, E. C., *Byzantine Silver Stamps* (Washington, 1962).
DOWNEY, Glanville, 'Justinian as a Builder', *Art Bulletin*, XXXII, pp. 262–3 (1950).
GRABAR, A., *Martyrium* (2 vols. Paris, 1943, 1946).
    'Le succès des arts orientaux à la cour byzantine sous les Macédoniens', *München Jahrbuch*, 3rd series, II (1951).
    'La Représentation de l'Intelligible dans l'Art Byzantin du Moyen Age', *Actes du VI. Cong. Int. d'Etudes Byzant.* (Paris, 1951).
    Byzantine Painting (Geneva, 1953).
    L'Iconoclasme Byzantin (Paris, 1957).
HAMILTON, R. W., *Khirbat al Mafjar* (Oxford, 1959).
KITZINGER, E., *Early Medieval Art in the British Museum* (London, 1940 and 1955).
    'The cult of Images in the Age before Iconoclasm,' *Dumbarton Oaks Papers*, VIII, pp. 85 et seq. (1954).
    'Byzantine Art in the Period between Justinian and Iconoclasm', *Proceedings of the XIth International Byzantine Congress* (Munich, 1958).
LEVI, D., *Antioch Mosaic Pavements* (Princeton, 1947).
MICHELIS, P. A., *An Aesthetic Approach to Byzantine Art* (London, 1955).

OATES, David, 'A Summary Report on the Excavations of the Byzantine Institute in the Karije Camii 1957–1958', *Dumbarton Oaks Papers*, XIV (1960).

PÄCHT, O., *Byzantine Illumination* (Oxford, 1952).

TALBOT RICE, David, *Byzantine Art* (London, 1954).

The Art of Byzantium (London, 1959).

SCHNEIDER, A. M., 'Das Martyrion der Hl. Euphemia', *Byzant. Zeitschrift*, XLII (1942–9).

TOYNBEE, J. M. C., 'Roma and Constantinopolis in Late Antique Art', *J.R.S.*, XXXVII (1947).

UNDERWOOD, P. A., in *Dumbarton Oaks Papers* (1955–60). First Preliminary Report on the Restorations in the Kariye Camii', *Dumbarton Oaks Papers*, IX and X, pp. 253 et seq.

'Second Preliminary Report', *Dumbarton Oaks Papers*, XI, pp. 172 et seq.

'Third Preliminary Report', *Dumbarton Oaks Papers*, XII, pp. 236 et seq. and pp. 267 et seq.

'Fourth Preliminary Report', *Dumbarton Oaks Papers*, XIII, pp. 187 et seq.

'The Deesis Mosaic in Kahrie Camii', *Studies in honour of A. M. Friend, Jnr.* (Princeton, 1955).

'Palaeologue Narrative Style and an Italianate Fresco of the Fifteenth Century in the Karije Camii', *Studies dedicated to W. A. Suidas* (London, 1959).

WARD-PERKINS, J. B. (and GOODCHILD, R. G.), 'The Christian Antiquities of Tripolitania', *Archaeologia*, vol. 45, pp. 1–82 (1953).

WARD-PERKINS, J. B., 'A new group of Sixth-Century Mosaics from Tripolitania', *Rivista di Archeologia Christiana*, pp. 183–95 (1958).

WEITZMANN, K., *Illustrations in Roll and Codex* (Princeton, 1947).

The Joshua Roll (Princeton, 1948).

Greek Mythology in Byzantine Art (Princeton, 1951).

The Fresco Cycle of Santa Maria di Castelseprio (Princeton, 1951).

Ancient Book Illumination (Cambridge, Mass., 1959).

WELLESZ, Emmy, *The Vienna Genesis.* (London, 1960).

Index

AGAPIUS, 55
Agathias, 3, 62-3, 67-8, 74, 77-8, 81, 92, 117
Agnellus, 62
Akropolites, George, 136, 146, 157
Alaric, 49
Alberti, Leon Battista, 31
Alexander the Great, 16, 148
Alexandria, viii, 6, 23, 26, 42-3, 53, 83, 86, 111
Alexios I Comnenos, 135
Alföldi, Dr, 57
Alp Arslan, Sultan, 134
Ammianus, 55
Amorian Emperors, vii, 103, 108-21, 131
Anastasius, Emperor, 49, 55, 65, 94-5
Ariadne, Augusta, 65
Anatolia, 83
Andronicus II Palaeologos, 136
Anthemius of Tralles, 25, 28, 30, 65, 67-9, 92, 114
Anthology, Palatine, 26, 72-3, 78, 112
Antioch, 77, 83, 111
Antipater of Sidon, 76
Antoniadis, Mademoiselle, xiii
Antonines, 12, 14-15
Antonios, Patriarch, 137
Apollonius of Perga, 69
    Conics, 69
Arabius Scholasticus, 63
Arcadius, Emperor, 57
Architecture, 3-4, 18, 25, 28, 31, 36, 62-3, 86, 92-3, 106-7, 111-12, 127, 151
Argentarius, Julianus, 69
Argyropoulos, 161
Argyros, Isaac, 28
    Method of Geodesy, 28

Aristotle and Aristotelianism, 2, 4, 55, 115-17, 120, 157
    Animalia, 157
    De Anima, 117
    Ethics, 157
    Metaphysics, 120
    Poetics, 4, 115
    Politics, 157
Arithmetic, 3-4, 25-6, 149
Armenia, 94-5, 109, 134
Asclepios of Tralles, 26
Asia Minor, 8, 49, 63, 95, 100, 109, 134-5, 142, 146
Asinou, 143
Aspar, 49
Astronomy, 3
Athens, xii-xiii, 20, 50, 73, 137, 145
    Byzantine Museum, xii-xiii, 145
    National Library, 137
Athos, Mount, xiii, 8, 110, 137, 140
Augustus, Emperor, 14-15
Aurelian, Emperor, 13

BAGHDAD, 128
Balbinus, Emperor, 13
Balkans, South, 63, 109
Bari, 134
Barker, Sir Ernest, xiii
Basil of Caesarea, 20
Basil I, Emperor, 108, 111-12, 120, 122
Basil II, Emperor, 111, 115, 131, 152
    Menologion, 115, 131, 152
Baynes, Professor Norman, xiii
Beckwith, John, xii-xiii
Belisarius, 65-6, 70
Benjamin of Tudela, 135
Berlin, 138
Bessarion, George, 161

Blemmydes, Nikephoros, 136, 157
Boiana, 137
Bowra, Sir Maurice, xiii
Brontochion, *see* Mistra
Brusa, 8
Buckler, Georgina and William, xiii
Byzantine Art (*See separate headings*)
History of, 1, 9–10, 49, 53, 142
Patrons of, 7, 44, 53–4, 64, 74–5, 86, 100, 110, 137, 139, 144–6, 148, 156, 161
Byzantium and Byzantines, 2, 7, 11–12, 20, 24, 32, 34, 49, 51, 53–4, 63, 70, 75, 90, 120, 127, 129, 135, 140, 145
Civil Service, 48, 52, 54–5, 66, 69–73, 76, 97, 133, 136–7, 139, 146, 160

CAIRO, 128, 133
Calixtus, 45
Callirhoe, 74
Cappadocia, 50, 60, 142–3, 145
Castelseprio, 11, 124
Catacomb Painting, 44–5
Caucasus, 63, 109
Cefalu, 10
Ceramics, 128–9
Cerularius, Michael, 132
Cherson, 102, 127
Chimay, 138
China, x, 6, 53, 87, 127
Chios, 131, 143
Nea Moni, 131, 143
Christianity, viii, 6–7, 12–13, 23–4, 39–47, 50, 52, 57–60, 70–2, 78–80, 84–6, 94–100, 103–7, 109–10, 126–8, 145, 147–8, 155
Christodoros, 55
Chrysopolis, 102
Classicism, 1–2, 4, 10, 12–14, 16–17, 20, 22–4, 27, 47,

49–50, 52–3, 61–2, 73, 91, 111, 115–16, 123–4, 131, 148
Claudius II, Emperor, 13, 56
Codices, Purple, 82–6, 123
Collingwood, R. G., 91
Colour, vii, 1, 5–6, 10, 17, 19–20, 26, 33–4, 36–7, 58, 63, 83, 87–90, 103, 118–21, 125, 129–30, 138, 142–50, 153–6, 159–60
Cometas the Cartularius, 112
Comnena, Anna, 2, 140, 146, 158
Alexiad, 2–4, 146
Comnenians, vii, xi, 126, 131, 133, 135–42, 144–6, 150, 156–8
Constantine I, Emperor, 12–14, 48–50, 52, 121
Constantine V, Emperor, 100, 102
Constantine VI, Emperor, 103
Constantine VII Porphyrogenitos, 111, 125
Constantine VIII, Emperor, 108
Constantine IX Monomachos, 108, 131
Constantine XI, Emperor, 7, 138
Constantinople, viii–xi, xiii, 2, 4–5, 7, 9–12, 17, 32, 48–9, 54, 57, 60, 62, 64, 67, 70, 73–4, 77, 83, 85, 87–8, 91, 94–5, 103, 109–13, 122, 124, 127–8, 131, 133, 135–40, 143–5, 148, 152, 154, 161
Churches of Constantinople:
Chora, viii, xiii, 4, 10, 17, 39, 54, 136, 138, 140, 144, 151–3, 159
Haghia Sophia, x–xi, xiii, 4–5, 10, 16, 25, 29, 35–6, 53, 62–3, 67, 69, 71, 87–91, 93, 112, 121, 123–4, 131, 137–8, 159
Nea, 112, 120, 132
Pammakaristos, 138
Constantius, Emperor, 57
Coptic Culture, 60, 94
Corfu, 8

Crete, 8, 128
Ctesiphon, 17
Cyprus, 138, 142–3
Cyrenaica, 86
    Qasr el Lebia, 86
Cyrene, 63
Cyril of Alexandria, 24, 62
Cyrus of Panopolis, 65

DAMASKINOS, MICHAEL, 8
Daphni, 5, 136, 143, 145, 150
Decius, Emperor, 13
Decorative Art, Secular and Re-
    ligious, 3, 8, 10–11, 38, 40,
    44–6, 57, 59–60, 63, 67, 69,
    74, 76, 78, 84, 86–7, 90–3,
    95–6, 100, 105, 112–13, 124–5,
    128–9, 131–2, 142–3, 148,
    153–4
Delos, 45
Delphi, 73
Demetrius of Philippi, 70
Demus, Dr Otto, 29
Denis of Fourna, 9
    Painter's Guide, 9
Diocletian, viii, 12–14, 48, 50, 57
Diogenes, Nikephoros, 3
Dios, 102
Drama, 2, 7, 126
    Mime, 126
Duccio, 9
Dukas, Empress Irene, 2, 4, 102–3,
    159
    Dukas (family), 146, 157
Dumbarton Oaks Collection, xii,
    138
Dura Europos, 40–2

EGYPT, 45, 63, 75, 94–5, 98, 111,
    124, 132–3
El Greco, 8
Eleusis, Mysteries at, 16
Emperors, East Roman (*see also*
    individual names), 162–4
    chronology of, 162–4
Enamels, ix, xi, 3, 11, 122, 129–31,
    144, 149, 156
Epictetus, 21
Epicurus, 123
Epirus, 137
Ethiopia, 83, 132
    Cusquam, 83
    Iteghe Mentuab, Empress, 83
Euclid, 29–33, 37, 68–9
    Catoptrica, 30, 36
    Elements, 37, 68–9
    Optics, 29, 33, 37
Eudoxia Ingerina, Empress, 108
Eugenianos, Niketas, 148
Eulalius, 69
Eunapios, 51
Euphrates, 40, 148
Euripides, 2, 124
Eusebius of Caesarea, 97
Eustathios of Thessalonika, 75, 158
Euthymios Zigabenos, 24, 158
Eutocius, 28, 69

FITZWILLIAM MUSEUM, Cam-
    bridge, xiii
Florence, 138
Florian, Emperor, 13
Frangopoulos, John, 54

GABRIEL the Prefect, 81
Galata, 143
Galla Placida, *see* Ravenna
Gallienus, Emperor, 13–17, 20
    Salonina, 14
    Saloninus, 14
Geminus of Rhodes, 5, 34
Genoa and Genoese, 139
Geometres, John, 5, 112, 147
Geometry, 3–5, 24–5, 28, 34, 67–8,
    112, 148–9
    Geodesy, 28–9, 112

Gerke, Dr F., 45
Gibbon, Edward, 9
Giotto, 9, 32, 152
Goblets, 11
Goths, 81
Grabar, Dr André, 19, 32
Gray, Basil and Nicolete, xiii
Greece, 9–10, 20, 23, 25, 43, 63, 109, 112, 115–16, 154, 158
Gregory Kentrokukuros, 102
Gregory Nazianzen, 20, 23, 122, 132
Gregory of Nyssa, 20, 23, 158
Gregory Palamas, 140
Grottaferata, 146

HADRIAN, Emperor, 2, 14–16
Hansa League, 139
Harmony, 5, 17, 26, 28, 37, 62, 142–61
Hellenism, 2, 15–16, 21, 32–4, 36, 38, 40, 43–5, 49, 56, 58–9, 61, 67, 70, 76, 78, 85, 90, 123–4, 127, 140, 143, 151, 155
Heraclius, Emperor, 95, 101
Heron of Alexandria, 27–8, 30
Hesychasm, 140
Hiereia, Council of, 101
Holl, Dr, 104
Homer, 2–3, 110, 124
    Iliad, 2
Hosios Loukas, xiii, 5, 124, 131, 142–3
Huns, 66
Huxley, George, xiii
Hymettos, 8
Hypatia, 28
Hypatius of Ephesus, 70

IAMBLICHUS, 26, 158
Iconoclasm, 93, 99–103, 117, 122–6, 129, 131
    Iconodules, 100–4, 115, 118, 122
Iconography, 7–9, 25, 35, 43, 47, 50, 57–8, 60, 74–6, 78, 81, 84, 98–9, 103, 105, 109, 120–1, 131, 144, 152
Ignatius the Magister, 125
Image and Picture, 1, 8, 32, 37, 81, 93–108, 117–18, 120–1, 124–5
India, 130
Indicopleustes, Cosmas, 80
    Christian Topography, 80
Irak, 154
Isidore of Miletus, 28, 69, 92–3, 114
Islam, x, 7, 95, 122, 127–9, 131
    Muhammad, 95
Italy, 8–9, 32, 64, 109, 123, 142, 153, 161
Ivories, 11, 58, 63, 82–3, 88, 128–31, 149

JAMES of Kokkinobaphos, 136–7
Jewellery, 3, 130, 138
    Caskets, 131
Jews and Judaism, 42
John of Cappadocia, 65–6
John Chrysostom, 6, 62, 132
John of Damascus, 24, 104, 118–19, 149, 157
John II Comnenos, Emperor, 137
John III Dukas Vatatzes, 156
John VI Cantacuzene, Emperor, 138
Julian, Emperor, 49–52, 97
Julianus the Prefect, 72, 76
Justin I, Emperor, 26, 65, 81
    Sophia, Empress, 81
Justinian, Emperor, vii, ix–x, 11, 28, 51–2, 58, 60, 62–78, 80–1, 85, 87–8, 92–4, 98, 107, 109, 121, 126, 130–1, 151
    Theodora, Empress, 65–6, 80–1, 86

KALLINIKOS the Cubicularius, 81
Karystos, 36
Khatzikis, Manuel Lascaris, 159
Konjica, 44

Kyriakides, Dr S. P., 146

LASCARID DYNASTY, 136
Lascaris, Theodore, 157, 161
Leningrad, ix, xii, 78, 138
  Hermitage Museum, ix, xii, 78, 138
Leo III the Isaurian, Emperor, 99–102
Leo V, Emperor, 102
Leo VI the Wise, Emperor, x, 16, 108, 111, 114, 123–4
Leontios the Scholastic, 72, 74, 76–7, 81
Leontius of Byzantium, 62, 115
Light, 1, 5, 19–20, 63, 117
Lincoln College, 152
Lindos, 45
Literature, 2, 22, 62, 95, 111, 123–4, 146, 156
Liturgy, ix, 2, 7, 24, 96, 106, 125, 158
Liutprand, Bishop of Cremona, 113
Livia, 14
Logistics, 25–8, 112, 149
London, xiii, 87, 115, 123, 126, 139
  British Museum, xiii, 87, 115, 123, 126
  Victoria and Albert Museum, xiii, 138
Longinus, 6, 143
Lucas, Christian, xiii, 52
Lydia, 55
Lydus, John, 54–5, 70

MACEDONIA, vii, x, 10, 70, 122–34, 142, 144, 151, 156
Macedonian Emperors, vii, 103, 108–21, 157
Macedonius the Consul, 63, 72
Mackail, Professor J. W., 116–17
Malacca, 139
Manuel I Comnenos, 135, 146

Manuel II Palaeologos, 137
Manuscript Illumination, viii, 33, 83–6, 115, 122–3, 126–7, 131, 136–7, 144, 151–2, 156
Manzikert (battle), 134
Marble-work, 35–7, 69, 76–7, 88–9, 132, 149
Marcus Aurelius, Emperor, 50
Marina the Singer, 74
Marinus the Prefect, 65
Mathematics, 1, 24–37, 39, 62, 67, 69, 112, 127, 149, 158
Maurice, Emperor, 65, 95
Mavrogordato, John, xiii
Maximian, Bishop, ix, 53, 83, 87
Maximus, Confessor, 158
Mechanics, 24–5, 27, 62–3, 67–8
Megaspilaeon, 159
Mesarites, Nikolaos, 132, 147–50
Mesopotamia, 63, 109
Metalwork, viii–ix, xi, 11, 57, 63, 72, 77, 87
Methodios of Olympos, 21, 26, 40–2
Metochites, Theodore, 54, 136, 138, 157–60
Metrodoros, 26
Michael, Abbot, 120
Michael of Ephesus, 157
Michael II the Amorian, 95, 125
Michael III, Emperor, 103, 108
Michael IV, Emperor, 108
Michael VIII Palaeologos, 136, 138
Michelis, Dr A., 31
Milan, viii, 17, 48, 139
  Brera Gallery, viii, 17
Miletus, 142
Millet, Gabriel, xiii, 10
Mistra, xi, xiii, 10, 54, 139–40, 145, 152, 154, 159, 161
  Churches:
    Brontochion, 154, 159
    Pantanassa, xi, xiii, 10, 54, 140,

155, 159
Peribleptos, xi, 10, 140, 145, 155
Monastic Communities, viii, xi, xiii, 5, 8, 10–11, 54, 91, 98, 110, 124, 131, 140, 142–3, 155
Monemvasia, 139, 154
Mongol Conquests, 138–9
Monophysites, 102
Monreale, xi, 151
Mosaics, x–xi, 3, 5, 7, 9–10, 16, 24, 29, 32–5, 37, 42, 54, 59, 63, 69, 76–7, 80, 86, 88–9, 91–2, 95, 100, 106–7, 119, 123, 126, 128, 131, 136, 138, 144, 147–52, 159
Moscow, xiii, 160
    Central Restoration Workshop, xiii
    Tretiakov Gallery, xiii
Music, 3, 5, 19, 26, 132
Myriokephalon, 135
Mysticism, 6–7, 22, 26, 140

NARRATIVE, 142, 145, 147–9, 151
Naukratios, 117
Nemesios of Emesa, 62, 149
Neo-Platonism, 12, 19–20, 32, 157–8
Nerez, 138, 144
Nicea, 71, 103, 105, 124, 136–7, 146, 157
    Council of, 103, 105
Nicholas Mysticus, 127–8
Nicomachus of Gerasa, 25–6
    Isagoge, 25
Nikephoros of Constantinople, 119–20, 157
Nikephoros II Phokas, 108, 111
Nilus the Scholastic, 76–7, 116–17
Number, theory of, 24–6, 28

OBOLENSKY, Dmitri, xiii
Ochrida, 124, 138

Optics, 1, 5, 24–5, 29–30, 36–7, 63, 68, 107, 150–3
Origen, 42–3
Osmanli Sultanate, 7, 157, 160
Ostrogoths, 49, 66

PACHYMERES, George, 26
Padua, 32
Paganism and Crypto-Paganism, 51, 96, 98, 109
Painting (*see also separate headings*), 2, 4–5, 8–9, 34, 44, 67, 73–4, 119–20, 123, 127–8, 142, 154, 159
Palaeologans, vii, 34, 135–42, 145–6, 148–9, 156–7, 159–60
Palermo, xi, 151
Palestine, 63, 95
Panel-painting, xii, 8–9, 33, 75, 98, 103, 119, 145, 156
Pantanassa, *see* Mistra
Pappus of Alexandria, 28–9
    Little Astronomy, 29–30
Parabiago, viii, 17
Paris, ix, xiii, 15, 58, 82, 84, 127, 136–7, 153, 161
    Bibliothèque Nationale, 82, 137
    Louvre, ix, xii–xiii, 15, 58
    Musée Guimet, xiii
Patmos, viii, xiii, 8, 143
Paulus Silentarius, 25, 35, 63, 75–6, 87, 90
Pedhoulas, 143
Pergamum, 73
Peribleptos, *see* Mistra
Persia and Persians, 7, 49, 56–8, 66, 81, 95, 129, 132, 139
    Khusru II, 95
    Sassanians, 49, 56–8, 82
Perspective, 1, 5, 19, 31–4, 150, 152
Peximenites, 102
Pheidias, 18
Philadelphia, 55

Philip, Emperor, 16
Philoponos, John, 26, 62, 98
Philosophy, 2, 13, 20, 24, 28, 51, 156–8, 160
Photios, 110–11, 128, 132
Phrygia, 50
Pindar, 73
Planudean Appendix, 72, 81–2, 117
Plato and Platonism, 2, 4, 6, 20–1, 23, 51, 55, 97–8, 116, 157–8
  Dialogues (various), 4, 21
Plethon, Gemistos, 141, 157–8
Plotinus, 4, 17, 19–21, 32, 63, 116, 158
  Enneads, 4, 17, 19–21, 116
Poetry, 5, 19, 73, 75–6, 78–9, 81–2, 112, 116–17, 119, 125, 141, 146–7
Porphyrios the Charioteer, 72–3
Porphyry the Philosopher, 17, 97, 158
Portraiture, 13–17, 72, 74–5, 96–7, 123, 159
Postumus, 15
Princeton University, 137
Probianus, 56
Probus, 13
Proclus, 5, 20, 26, 28, 30, 32, 34, 55, 62, 116, 119, 158
  Euclid, 5, 34
Procopius, 62, 67, 70–1, 86, 89–90, 92–3
  Buildings, 71, 86–7, 89–90, 92–3
Prodromos, Theodore, 146
Prudentius, 51
Psellos, Michael, 28, 132–3, 156, 158–9
Pseudo-Dionysius, 62, 119, 158
Pupienus, Emperor, 13
Pythagoras, 26, 158

Qaranleq, 142
Qeledjlar, 142

Quintillus, Emperor, 13

Ragusa, 139
Ravenna, ix–x, 7, 9, 36, 41, 48, 53, 59, 62, 64, 79, 87, 135
  'Mausoleum of Galla Placida', 36, 41, 58, 91
  Churches:
  Neon, 59
  San Vitale, x, 7, 36, 39, 62–3, 69, 79–80, 88, 90–1
Religion, 7, 12, 21, 23, 57, 70–1, 84, 94, 97–8, 140, 145
  Religious Art, 6–10, 12, 16–17, 23, 38–40, 43–4, 59–60, 70, 78–81, 84, 87, 93, 95, 106–7, 112, 124, 127–9, 131, 142–3, 150–1, 158
Rhetoric, 21, 132–3
Rhineland, 139
Rhythm, 3, 5–6, 8, 17–18, 33, 39, 58, 89, 122, 124–5, 144
Romanos (poet), 62
Romanos I Lekapenos, 108
Romanos II, Emperor, 108
Romanos III Argyros, Emperor, 133
Romanos IV, Emperor, 134
Rome and Roman Empire, 1–2, 6–7, 12–14, 22, 28, 48–9, 51–2, 56, 58–61, 75, 95, 108, 110–11, 128, 133, 135, 137, 160–1
  Vatican, 138
Rossano, 84
Rublev, Andrei, 39
Rufinus the Domesticus, 72
Rumania, 154
Russia, ix, 4, 154

Sabratha, 11, 54
Sant' Angelo in Formis, 145
Saracens, 128

Sarcophagi, 13, 15–16, 45, 58, 123
Seljuks, 134–5
Severus, Alexander, 13
Severus, Septimus, 12
Sicily, 64, 135
Sinai, Mount (Monastery of St Katherine), xiii, 11, 54, 91, 98
Skenography, 5, 30–1, 34, 151
Sopocani, 137
Soteriou, M., xiii, 10
Spain, 51, 64, 139
Sparta, xi, 10, 154
Statuary and Sculpture, viii, 2, 5, 20, 49, 56–7, 67, 72–3, 81, 97, 123, 128
Stewart, Cecil, xii–xiii
Stilicho, 49
Stoicism, 20–1, 50, 158
Strygowski, Professor, 58
Sudan, 130
Symbolism, 7, 26, 32, 38–47, 81, 90, 92, 95, 99, 106–7
Symmetry, 1, 4, 17–18, 58, 91–2, 150
Asymmetry, 44, 150
Syria, 60, 63, 83, 94–5, 109, 111

Tacitus, Emperor, 13
Tak i Bostan, 82
Talbot Rice, Professor D., 10, 130
Tcharegli, 142
Tertullian, 46
Textiles, 11, 58, 63, 87–8, 128, 131, 149
Theodoric the Ostrogoth, 49
Theodore of Studios, 92, 101–2, 117, 157
Theodoret, 62
Theodoros of Caesarea, 115, 120
Theodosius, Bishop, 105
Theodosius I, Emperor, ix, 49–52, 56–7
Theodosius II, Emperor, 91
Theon of Alexandria, 28, 30

Theophano, Empress, 108
Theophilus, Emperor, 103, 113, 122, 125, 127–8
Thessalonika, xii, 10, 33, 60, 139, 143, 145, 161
Thessaly, 89
Thomas Magister, 74, 81, 146
Thrace, 109
Tmolos, Mount, 55
Tokale Kilisse, 142
Torcello, viii, xi, 10, 35, 39, 145
Trade Routes, 127, 133, 135, 139
Trebizond, 10, 137, 139, 154
Trier, 48
Tripolitania, 11
Tzanes, Manuel, 8

Underwood, Dr Paul, xii–xiii, 10

Valentinian II, Emperor, 51, 57
Vandals, 66
Venice, viii–xi, xiii, 8, 111–12, 122, 135, 139, 161
Byzantine Institute, xiii
San Marco, viii–xi, xiii, 122
Vienna, 82, 84–5
da Vinci, Leonardo, 31
Vitruvius, 36

Wall-paintings, viii, xi, 8–11, 33, 35, 72, 86, 90, 95, 103, 119, 123, 137–8, 142–3, 152–5
Wellesz, Emmy and Egon, xiii
Whittemore, Professor Thomas, xii–xiii, 10
Wirth, Dr Fritz, 44

Zante, 8
Zoe, Empress, 108
Zoticus, 55